With LOVE, Bev

A COURAGEOUS JOURNEY OF HEALING

BEVERLY DIFFERDING

GANDER PUBLISHING, PALO ALTO, CALIFORNIA & RUTLAND, VERMONT

PUBLISHED IN 1994.

LIBRARY OF CONGRESS CATALOG NUMBER: 93-81315

ISBN 0-9639586-1-5

PRINTED IN THE UNITED STATES OF AMERICA

COVER DESIGN BY BECCA SMIDT

GANDER PUBLISHING INC.
553 THAIN WAY, PALO ALTO, CALIFORNIA, 94306

Dedication

*This book is dedicated to my family
for their love, time, and faith.*

To those who helped me recover:

*The paramedics at the accident,
Dr. Farsad (abdominal surgery),
Dr. Oygar (back surgery),
Dr. Freiha (kidney surgery),
Drs. Thompson, Miller, and
Slobodian (rehabilitation),
Dr. Rinsky (Harrington rod surgery),
Dr. Garfield (chiropractic therapy),
and Diana Stumm and
Bob White (physical therapy).*

*To the hundreds of friends who
shared their love and their prayers, gave blood,
and sent flowers, books, cards, and letters.*

*And to Mary Wright Shaw
who encouraged me to write this story.*

Introduction

I did not die.

This book tells of the horror of being in a near-fatal automobile accident, the tragedy of losing dear friends, and the obstacles that paraplegic and quadriplegic patients must overcome to survive. It is about my recovery, against what medical professionals said were tremendous odds.

Despite my massive injuries — my spinal cord was completely severed, and I suffered other serious internal injuries — I refused "to get used to" my new condition.

As I wrote this book, I recalled past events that at the time made no sense to me. Now these pieces are fitting together like a puzzle. It started with a dream I had when I was nine years old. I believe it was then that I was first told of the trauma I would encounter 40 years later that would change my life forever.

In retrospect, it was as if I was being prepared for the accident. I think this explains why it has not made me angry or hateful and why I've never had problems talking about it.

Most of us who have encountered tragedies ask ourselves if we could have done anything to prevent them. There are always the "What ifs." I believe that some things in our lives are preordained. Of course, we still have some choices and control.

After the accident, in spite of massive injuries, I made an important choice: I chose to live.

I believe others can learn from my experiences, and not accept some doctor's opinion that progress is impossible.

This book is not only about my accident, the pain, and the frustration. It is about spiritual strength, courage, and love: love that I felt for others and that they felt for me. Love made miracles happen.

With this book I hope to touch the hearts of those who have lost faith and given up. No matter what our problems are — whether physical, mental or spiritual — I believe we have the power within ourselves to overcome them.

Contents

Introduction   vii

1. The Accident   1

2. Before The Accident   7
In The Beginning / Someone New / Egypt / Psychic Healing

3. Palm Springs   27
A Trip to Palm Springs / At Home / Emergency Surgery
Deciding to Live / Back Surgery / Some Good Things

4. Stanford Medical Center   57
Intensive Care Ward / Intermediate Care Ward
Kidney Surgery / Looking Forward to Rehab

5. Valley Medical Center   79
Valley Second Floor / Penny / Awaiting Surgery
Bleeding / The Air Bed / Awaiting Rehab

6. Rehabilitation   109
Rehab at Last / Therapy Begins / The Schedule
The X-Rated Movie / Mary / Roommates / The Nurses
The Mirror / In a Car Again / Standing / The Kidney Test
Exercise Classes / Ben / A Fun Weekend / Panic
Outside / The Parallel Bars / The Final Test / Leaving

7. Home   179
Home at Last / Therapy / Braces / A Return to Valley
On My Own / Thyme / A Spirit Guide / Visualization

8. Rod Surgery   205
Getting Worse / Agonizing Pain / To the Hospital
Home Awaiting Surgery / Surgery / Recovery
Going Home / Memory Loss

9. The Car   237
10. The Driver Who Hit Us   249
11. The Quake   255
12. The Move   263
Epilogue   271

1

The Accident

1

The Accident

Suddenly, the driver, Sharon, exclaimed, "Oh, my God!"

I looked up to see a white pick-up truck coming across the median strip, straight at us. I caught a glimpse of a man in the driver's seat before impact. In an instant the truck hit us head-on. Tires screeched and metal crunched against metal for what seemed like a terrifying eternity. Windows exploded. Shattered glass from the front windshield floated toward me. Everything happened in slow motion, as if time had expanded. (I had sometimes experienced this same feeling during an intense game of tennis, where the ball would seem to slow down and my racket glide soundlessly through the air before making contact. I've since talked to other accident victims who say they felt the same way — beyond fear — when they realized what was happening. Is this the way human nature deals with situations too terrifying to comprehend? I don't know.)

For those moments that I was conscious throughout this experience, I felt dreadfully calm.

I was hurtled against the front seat as the car lurched out of control. The force of the crash pushed the front seat back against my knees, trapping my legs and feet under it, cutting them in multiple places. Finally, the car stopped moving. Silence.

"My God, what's happening?" I thought.

Although my eyes were open, I couldn't see. There was total darkness. And although I knew we had been hit, I could feel no pain. As I listened, I heard soft moaning coming from Gerry. Then I realized I was moaning, too, and I thought I could hear the same sounds coming from the front seat. It sounded as though we were all breathing in unison: in and out, in and out. As each breath was softly released, we moaned, as if in gentle harmony. I will never forget that sound.

"Dear God," I thought, "Help us."

Then Gerry's head fell onto my shoulder.

"Gerry," I asked, "are you all right?"

She didn't respond.

My right hand was lying on my stomach, and I could feel something happening; my abdomen was swelling. I knew I had to unbuckle my seat belt. As I did this, I leaned against Gerry. I tried to move away from her, but I could only move my arms. I still had no pain, but I had no feeling in the lower half of my body. I managed to raise my right hand to feel for the window and realized that the glass was shattered. I put my hand through the broken window and held onto the roof of the car to try to pull myself upright, but I couldn't do it.

Then I heard Gerry vomit. I could feel a warm, thick liquid flowing down my left arm. I thought it was probably blood. Then Gerry stopped moaning.

"Oh, Gerry, don't die," I pleaded. But I knew she was dead.

Then I was aware of noises outside the car. Although I hadn't heard sirens or emergency vehicles approach, I heard footsteps on crushed glass as people hurried toward the car.

"Try not to move," a voice told me. Another voice at the front of the car said, "The driver's D.O.A."

"No, Sharon, not you, too!" I cried. I wanted to escape from the horrible scene, although I still felt no physical pain. I prayed, "Dear Jesus, please let me either pass out or let me leave my body until this is over. Don't make me stay here."

Then I felt a hand touch my right hand, which was still holding onto the outside of the car.

"You're going to be fine," a voice said. "We'll have you out in no time." I heard other people talking. A voice asked me, "Were you wearing your seat belt?"

"Yes," I said, "I just unbuckled it because I felt my abdomen swelling."

"Okay, sweetie," the voice said. "A few more minutes and you'll be out."

"Please don't let go of my hand," I cried. I still wasn't in pain, but I couldn't see, and I didn't want to be left alone.

"Don't worry, I won't," the voice reassured me.

Later I found out it was one of the paramedics who was holding my hand and talking to me. He kept telling me everything would be all right, and kept me calm as other paramedics used the Jaws of Life to pry me out of the car.

Finally, he told me what I was longing to hear. "Okay, sweetheart, we're going to pull you out. First I'm going to put a neck brace on you for your own protection."

During the next few minutes I faded in and out of consciousness as a brace was put on my neck, I was placed on a stretcher, and lifted into the ambulance. In the ambulance I heard a man's voice yelling and swearing at the paramedics to give him something for his pain. It had to be the man who had hit us, killed two of my friends, critically injuring another and myself. In the ambulance, the same paramedic sat down next to me and continued to hold my hand.

I asked, "Do you have a pencil and paper?"

"Yes," he replied.

"Would you please call my husband in Los Altos?"

I gave the paramedic John's name and phone number and heard another paramedic say, "She's really alert." Then he said, "Damn! I can't get a pulse on her! Do we have a destination yet?"

"No," said the ambulance driver.

"If we don't get her to a hospital soon, we'll lose her!" said the other paramedic.

When I heard that, I felt an enormous sense of relief. So I was going to die. I smiled, closed my eyes, thanked the Lord, and told Him I was ready.

Before
The Accident

2

In The Beginning

In 1946 I received my first Holy Communion at the Catholic church two blocks from home. Afterward, Mom, Dad, and a few relatives celebrated the event.

My godparents gave me a beautiful miniature altar. When it was plugged in, candles lighted on the altar. It reminded me of the altar at church. I loved it. It made me feel very holy. Every night I knelt before it and said my prayers before I went to bed. One night I had a beautiful dream. Although I was only nine and a half, I remember it clearly.

I was skipping along a narrow paved path. In the distance I saw a large iron gate. As I approached, I saw a long snake lying across the path. To continue I would have to jump over it. I hesitated. I felt I had nothing to fear, so I jumped over the snake and opened the gate.

The path led to an impressive old church, made of wood, with carvings of lovely angels above the door. I walked inside. The interior was the most wonderful sight I'd ever seen. The ceiling was high, but you could see the beautiful paintings on it. Along the sides were lovely stained glass windows. As I walked toward the altar, I was aware that I was alone in the church. The beauty and the stillness gave me a serene feeling.

Near the front, I sat in a pew. I knelt and made the sign of the cross. I reverently folded my hands and looked at the altar. On one side was a statue of Jesus. As I admired it, the statue began to move. I realized Jesus was coming toward me. I could see his hair, beard, and red cloak clearly, but his face was blurred. I knew He was smiling at me. He came to the pew in front of me, sat, and faced me. He placed his hand on mine. I could feel His touch. It was gentle and warm. He talked to me.

I awoke with a start. I was frightened. I couldn't remember what Jesus had said to me. I jumped out of bed and ran to tell Mom about the dream. After I told her everything, she said that it was a beautiful dream and I shouldn't be frightened.

My elementary school years were unpleasant. I was an only child and dependent on my mother. I was shy, and other children picked on me. I wasn't accepted by them. I felt excluded, as if I were on the outside looking in. I watched and didn't participate.

When I was thirteen, I watched one of my cousins pantomiming Al Jolson's *Mammy* for the family. She was dressed in a tux and had black makeup on her face. I thought she was wonderful. I wanted her to do it over and over. I watched intently. I tried to imitate everything she did. For the first time, I had found something I wanted to do.

My freshman year I signed up for the talent show. I wanted to mime Al Jolson. Mom bought one of his records for me. With my phonograph playing, I practiced for hours lipsynching with his voice. Although I was shy, I knew I would be able to go on stage. With makeup I could hide my face and be someone else.

After my successful performance, many students talked to me, even some who didn't know me. Then I began to blossom. I found it easier to talk to people. At last, I felt accepted.

The remainder of high school was fun. I performed at class rallies, continually miming new characters. Jerry Lewis was easy to imitate, and I enjoyed looking and acting goofy. I added Stan Freberg and Jane Powell. Students enjoyed my acts. I was considered talented and popular. In my sophomore year I was voted student body treasurer. In my junior and senior years I was a cheerleader. High school was one of my favorite times.

When I was a senior, I met the man who would be my first husband. He was two years ahead of me, a sophomore at San Francisco State. Soon after I graduated, we were married. I was much too young. We spent seventeen rather uneventful years together. Before the children were born, I worked in a bank. The two good things from the marriage were sons, Gary and Ken. I stopped working until the boys were old enough to go to school. Then I took up tennis. I fell in love with the game. I wished I had started before I was thirty years old.

In our fifteenth year of marriage I sensed my husband was going with someone else. I told him of my feelings and asked him if he was seeing someone. He tried to reassure me that it was my imagination. I desperately wanted to believe him. I later discovered that my intuition was right; my husband was having an affair. If only I had listened to my feelings, I would have spared myself two painful years trying to ignore what I knew was true. I was hurt because he had betrayed me. I was angry because he had lied to me. I was confused because I thought I had done everything he wanted me to do. I didn't know what I had done wrong. I was afraid of being on my own. I had lived eighteen years with my parents and seventeen with my husband. I didn't know how to live alone.

After two weeks of crying, I pulled myself together and made some decisions. I had to think of my boys. I wasn't going to waste more time or energy on my husband. There was no way I could live with someone who had deceived me. I could never trust him again.

I told him to leave the house. Two weeks later he was served with divorce papers.

I faced the biggest change in my life. We had to sell our home. I had to look for an apartment for my sons and me. I hadn't realized how difficult that would be. Many times I thought I had found an apartment or duplex, only to find the landlords wouldn't rent to a divorcee with eight- and ten-year-old boys. For the first time I experienced discrimination.

My time and patience grew short. I not only needed a place to live, I needed a job. My alimony and child support were $450 a month, just about what it cost for a two-bedroom apartment.

I found a job at a bank. One of my co-workers was getting married and would be leaving a duplex that she had been renting. She offered to talk to her landlord to see if I could rent it after she left. I was so excited when I learned the duplex was ours. It had two bedrooms, a bath, a kitchen, and a small living room. It wasn't great, but it was mine. For the first time I was on my own.

I worked at the bank from 9:30 to 3:30. I was home soon after the boys arrived home from school. I started dating some of the men that I had met through tennis. After so many years, it was strange to be dating again.

3

Someone New

I met John, a medical doctor, at the tennis courts. He was a good tennis player, far better than I, but we enjoyed playing tennis together. He had an unhappy marriage and had stayed with his wife for the good of his two daughters. He finally decided that he had to get a divorce. He is quiet, and I'm an extrovert, but we have fun together. We're both Scorpios. Our love is beautiful. I call him my soul mate. I don't think I could love anyone more than I love John.

In 1974 we married and moved into a nice home in Los Altos. We had some problems, the ones people encounter when they remarry and children are involved. A long time passed before John's girls accepted me and my boys accepted John.

About our third year of marriage, I developed insomnia. I would fall asleep but couldn't stay asleep for more than four hours. I became irritable. I went to a physician who prescribed sleeping pills. That worked for a month or so, and then I again had trouble sleeping. I tried a different physician who gave me a different drug which again worked for a short time and then I again had insomnia. This went on for a year. When Seconal, a strong sleeping pill, stopped working, I started doubling up on them. One night John noticed me taking three of them. He was furious.

"You've got to stop taking pills and see a doctor." I told him it wouldn't do any good. No one knew what to do for me. When I went to the doctor again, he told me I needed to see a psychiatrist. Since I loved my parents and had had a loving childhood, I didn't think that would help, but I made an appointment.

The psychiatrist told me I had to quit taking the pills. He said that Seconal suppresses dreams, and I probably hadn't dreamed normally for months. I could expect nightmares for at least five weeks. I thought it might not be too bad to have nightmares if I could sleep. After two more visits to the psychiatrist, I decided he couldn't help me. He was right about the nightmares. They were so bad I didn't want to fall asleep. They stopped after a month.

My insomnia continued. I was depressed and found it hard to concentrate.

One evening, as I watched my son playing little league baseball, I heard one of the mothers say she had used hypnosis to quit smoking. I asked her about hypnosis and if she thought it might help me. She thought that it could and gave me the name of the hypnotist, Paul.

I was hesitant. All I knew about hypnosis was what I had seen in the movies. I was desperate, so I called Paul and made an appointment. I arrived to find that his office was in his home. He seemed nice, and I felt comfortable talking to him. He had no doubt that he could help me. He would help me to help myself. I liked that. I learned self-hypnosis in three sessions. For the first time I felt I would get better. During my last visit, he told me I was very intuitive and asked if I wanted to develop my psychic awareness.

"Heavens, no. I don't want to know what's going to happen before it happens."

He laughed and dropped the subject. He reminded me that if I wanted to improve, I must practice hypnosis every day.

When I left his office, I wondered why he thought I was intuitive. I should have asked. As I thought of unusual things that had happened to me, I remembered my dream of Jesus.

Then I remembered dreams of my grandfather. He and I had a special relationship. Although we spent little time together, we were close in spirit. The day before he died, in January of 1967, I had talked to him and he seemed fine. The next day I learned he was in the hospital. He died later that night. At his wake, as I saw him lying in the coffin, I cried uncontrollably.

When I came home that night, I was upset because I hadn't been able to say good-bye to him.

When I went to bed, I thought about him.

"Nono, I am going to miss you so," I said aloud. "If only I could have said good-bye to you."

A large picture hanging on the wall fell to the floor. I nearly jumped off the bed.

"Please, Nono," I said, "If you're here, don't appear to me. I'd die of fright. If you have something to say to me, come to me in my dreams."

That seemed less scary to me than to actually see his spirit. I don't know why.

That night I dreamed I was sitting with him on a park bench. It was a beautiful, peaceful day. The trees and grass were bright green, and the sky a soft blue. I was amazed at how well he looked. He smiled and spoke to me in Italian. Although I don't speak or understand Italian, I knew what he was saying. He told me not to be sad for him. He was the happiest he had ever been.

Several months later I again dreamed of my grandfather. Although my dreams usually are in beautiful colors, this one was in black and white.

He called, "Beverly, Beverly."

At first I didn't recognize him, because he was sitting in a wheelchair. That was odd, because he always had been strong and healthy.

I ran to him and asked, "What's wrong?"

He handed me a heart-shaped locket.

"Beverly, I'm so sorry I couldn't do more for you."

I didn't know what he meant.

Then he was gone.

I thought about these dreams and wondered why I remembered them. I didn't think my dreams had anything to do with being intuitive. I decided not to think about it. I would concentrate on hypnosis.

I worked on self-hypnosis daily. Paul had taught me well. I cured my insomnia and improved my sinus condition. I was able to cure a few aches and pains.

I wasn't as faithful in practicing my hypnosis as I thought I would be. Once I started sleeping through the night, my energy level was high, and I returned to my usual busy lifestyle.

About eight months later I had a unique experience. One morning, after I awoke, I lay in bed. I was staring at the ceiling, when a small white spot appeared. It slowly enlarged to the size of a TV screen, and a picture began to form. I could see the body of a small person lying on the street near my house. A man in a white shirt was leaning over it. I was apprehensive, as if something bad had happened.

A week later I heard a siren in front of my house. When I went outside to see what was happening, I saw a young boy lying on the street. He had been riding his bike when he was hit by a car. Leaning over him was a paramedic, wearing a white jacket. It was just as I had pictured it. I called Paul to ask what he thought of my experience.

Paul wasn't surprised. He said I was intuitive. He recommended that I read a book called "Explore Your Psychic World" by Olga Worrall. He told me of classes I could take at Foothill College about psychic awareness.

I spent several months reading as many books as I could about the psychic world, and took several classes on the subject. Meditation was frequently mentioned and seemed to be the door to the psychic world. I tried meditating, but I didn't have the patience to sit still. I couldn't concentrate. My mind wandered. I lost interest in it.

About ten months later I again had visions similar to my previous one. Images formed, and the colors were sharp. I didn't know what I was seeing and I was uneasy. I didn't want to see them. When the white light formed, I would shut my eyes tightly and shake my head until the light disappeared.

Life was moving smoothly. My family and I were happy. I used hypnosis occasionally, mostly for my tennis game. It helped me win some close matches.

In 1981 I had another bizarre experience. I was in bed and had just fallen asleep. Suddenly I sat up. I found myself at the foot of the bed, watching myself sleeping soundly. I was surprised, but I didn't panic. As I looked around the room, I realized that I was floating. I felt as light as a feather. I decided to go into another room, and, in a split second, I was there. I could rapidly zip from place to place. I was enjoying myself until I became aware that what I was experiencing was unusual. I became frightened.

"God is with me. No harm can come to me," I repeated over and over with my arms outstretched.

I noticed that the sound of my voice was very different, as if it were coming from deep in my throat. Repeating the phrase reassured me. Warm love surrounded me and became stronger and stronger, more beautiful than anything I had ever experienced. I felt peaceful and at one with God. From that time on, I knew I would never fear death. As I was absorbing the overwhelming love, I heard Ken calling, "Mom, Mom." I zipped back to my bed. As I entered my body, I felt a shock and heard a click.

"What, Ken?" I answered, opening my eyes.

There was no answer. I went into his room. He was asleep.

That experience, which changed my attitude about death, would be important to me later.

The next day I called Paul to tell him all about my new adventure. He told me I had had an out-of-body experience and tried to explain it to me. He recommended more books for me to read.

When I read about other people's out-of-body experiences, I was surprised to find that the way their spirit left their body was similar to mine. Apparently, some people can leave their body at will. Even though it was a beautiful experience that I'll never forget, I wasn't sure I wanted to learn to do it at will. I felt it had more meaning when it just happened. I've had no other out-of-body experiences. If it happens again, I won't be frightened, I'll enjoy it.

Because I was curious about the unknown, I thought I would enjoy taking a class titled *How to Meet Your Spirit Guide*.

Our teacher asked us to close our eyes and relax. The technique was similar to that Paul had taught me. The teacher told us to visualize a quiet place, a place where we would be comfortable. We were to imagine our own psychic room. We could decorate it any way we wanted. He asked us to picture a large comfortable chair in the room and a door on the other side of the room. When we were ready, we were to sit in our imaginary chair and ask our spirit guide to enter. I followed the directions, but didn't expect anything to happen. To my surprise the door opened. There was not one, but two figures coming toward me. As they approached, I realized one was my grandfather. I didn't recognize the woman with him. I was so happy to see him, I began to cry. It had been ten years since I'd seen him. He was happy to see me. I wanted to talk to him, but all I could do was cry. There were so many questions I wanted to ask him. I wanted to be introduced to the woman with him. I felt I knew her.

I heard the teacher say it was time to leave our psychic rooms. I didn't want to leave; I wanted to stay with my grandfather. As I returned to the classroom, I was still crying. It was a wonderful experience. It felt real.

Later, I described my experience to Mom. She said that the woman with my grandfather fit the description of her mother, my grandmother, who had died when my mother was born. My mother had only seen a picture of her. Everything about the woman, including her dress, was like the picture Mom had seen.

For awhile, I practiced visiting my psychic room, but my grandfather and grandmother never reappeared. There have been times when I've felt my grandfather's presence.

I believe he will always be close by.

4

Egypt

In 1983, my friend, Betty, asked if I wanted to take a psychic awareness class with her at DeAnza College, given by a famous psychic. I was interested, and we went.

Our instructor was witty and we enjoyed her class. She was planning to take a tour group to Egypt and encouraged students to sign up. Betty and I thought it would be fun. When I went home and told John about the trip, he thought we should go. By the time I called Betty, she and Bill had decided to go.

As we prepared for the trip, I felt uneasy. My intuition told me I shouldn't go. I tried to ignore the feeling, but it persisted. I decided to see a psychic that I had known and trusted for years, to learn whether she thought I should take the trip. She assured me I would have a wonderful time, and, for awhile, I believed her.

We continued to prepare for our trip, getting visas, passports, and clothes we would need. I began to feel uneasy again. One week before the trip, I decided to talk to one more psychic. I wanted reassurance that it was all right to go on the trip, and possibly a reason for why I felt I shouldn't go. I don't know what I would have done if one of them had said I shouldn't travel. The third psychic agreed that I would have a great trip.

At last it was time to go. Since all three psychics had told me everything would be fine, I decided not to worry.

We arrived in Egypt safely. Our first day in Cairo we were to visit the Great Pyramid. Our teacher told us it was a mystical place, and some people had had spiritual awakenings inside the pyramid. I was looking forward to a wonderful experience.

When we arrived at the Great Pyramid, our tour guide warned us that, if we were claustrophobic, we shouldn't go in. Even though I am, I was determined to go in anyway.

"I didn't come all this way to sit in the bus," I whispered.

When we got off the bus, everyone was impressed by the pyramid's size. I'd seen pictures of the pyramid. None of them did it justice. Many people were admiring the sight and taking pictures. Some of the Egyptians were offering camel rides.

We waited in a long line to enter the pyramid. I used the time for self-hypnosis to control my fear. I took deep breaths and told myself to relax.

The passageway inside was only about four feet high and full of people. The air was foul and hot.

When we reached the upper chamber, it was full of tourists. I was disappointed. There would be no spiritual awakening for me. I only wanted to get out of there.

The second day of our trip, the tour group went to the Cairo Museum. John and I developed dysentery. We didn't know where we had picked it up. We had drunk only the hotel's bottled water.

The next morning I had severe abdominal cramps and stayed in my room. When John returned from the Cairo Museum, we decided to take a nap.

John awoke yelling, "What a nightmare! We've got to get out of here."

"It's only a dream, John. Nothing bad is going to happen. Try to relax and go back to sleep."

I thought about the feelings I had had before the trip. Now the trip wasn't fun. I thought we would be better in a few days and would be able to continue the trip.

I went to the bathroom again. My cramps were bad. I was sick and felt faint.

The next thing I remember was John saying, "Babe, talk to me."

I couldn't answer. I realized I was lying on the bathroom floor with John bending over me.

I thought, "I'm ready to die if God wants me. I'm ready."

I slowly turned my head to look at John, who was trying to get me to talk.

"What happened?" I asked.

"You fainted and fell on your face. You hit your forehead on the marble sink. It's split wide open."

There was blood all over. I could feel it running down my face. John lifted me, carried me into the bedroom, and put me on the bed.

There was no doctor in the hotel at that time, but one finally arrived. John held my hand as the doctor cleaned the wound. They could see my skull. It took eight stitches to close the wound. John told the doctor I had dysentery and had fainted.

He replied, "Don't drink the bottled water. Drink only fluids that come from a can or have been boiled."

When I tried to sit up, I fell backward. I had vertigo. John wanted to get me home as soon as possible. Our three week vacation lasted four days. After I was home, I found my nose was broken. Months passed before the vertigo disappeared.

I learned an important lesson, or maybe I should say I received my spiritual awakening in another way. I shouldn't rely on others to make decisions for me. I should trust my intuition.

5

Psychic Healing

In January 1987 a friend asked if I would take a psychic healing class with her.

"Why not?" I thought.

The thought of being able to heal others was exciting. Several psychics had told me that I was a channel for healing. I'd see what I could learn.

I enjoyed the class. The teacher told us how important dreams could be, and that we were to keep a journal by our bed and write down our dreams. We took turns telling about our dreams in class. Most of the time we did hands-on healing.

One night when I arrived home from class, John was in bed with a migraine that was causing numbness in two fingers. Kidding, I asked if he wanted me to do a healing on him.

"Why not? It can't hurt," he said.

I did everything I had been taught in class. Much to our surprise, his headache and numbness were gone in minutes.

"This is great, Babe. It worked. I don't have any pain."

"I know. I've got your headache."

I had to lie down for twenty minutes before the headache left me. Whenever I did a healing, my hands would get extremely hot and turn red. I realized I wasn't doing the healing; I was only a channel. Unfortunately, I either took on the other person's pain or lost most of my energy. The teacher said I was like a sponge, soaking up everyone's pain. She taught me how to protect myself with the white light of Christ. I tried a few more healings, but I still absorbed some of the pain. I decided that healing was not for me.

In April 1987 I dreamed I was in a big warehouse with many people I didn't know. A woman approached me with a gardenia. I held out my hands, and she placed the flower in them. As I looked at the petals, I noticed they were turning brown. I was sad that the flower was dying. Then new petals began to form. They grew, and the flower began to open. When the flower was in full bloom, it felt heavy. I looked closely at it and saw a newborn baby in the center of the flower. The people in the warehouse walked toward me, calling me a healer.

(As I look back, I realize that the warehouse was the hospital. The people there were the patients. The flower that died and then bloomed with the baby inside was me. I was reborn.)

Palm Springs

6

A Trip to Palm Springs

March 19, 1987

As I opened my eyes, sunlight shone through the curtains. I had slept poorly and was more tired than when I went to bed. I tried to focus on the clock. It was only 7:20; I had time to rest a little longer.

As I lay on my back staring at the ceiling, a small circle of light appeared. It grew as large as a TV screen, and a picture began to form. My heart beat faster. I wanted to close my eyes. I was frightened, but I decided to be brave and look carefully.

On the screen was a stretcher holding someone covered with an olive drab blanket. Two paramedics carried the stretcher to an ambulance and placed it inside. I didn't recognize the road with brown land on either side and no homes or stores. Then, I was above the scene, looking down. When I thought it might be me on the stretcher, I was filled with terror. Why had I let that vision come through? I couldn't watch any more. I closed my eyes tightly till the vision disappeared.

I was upset. I didn't want to go to a psychic healing seminar with two of my friends. But if I went, the psychic could tell me what she thought of my vision. I wondered if she would know more than I did. I knew what I saw, what I felt, and what I thought it meant. I didn't know what to do. Maybe I should forget it, maybe it was someone else on the stretcher, or maybe it was only a dream.

After my morning coffee, I decided to go. I heard a horn honk. Lynn had come to pick me up.

At the seminar my friends noticed I wasn't my usual talkative self.

"Are you all right?" asked Lynn. "You seem awfully quiet."

I told them about the vision. They tried to reassure me that I wasn't the one on the stretcher. I wanted to believe that, but it was difficult. In a few days I forgot about the experience.

April 26, 1987

It was a beautiful morning with sunlight shining through my bedroom window. Outside the birds were singing in the olive tree. Mornings like this make it easy to get out of bed. Today would be a special day, the beginning of a four-day vacation. Dee had a condo in Palm Springs and had invited Sharon, Gerry, and me to join her there for tennis, golf, swimming, and sunbathing. What a life! Sometimes I almost felt guilty.

"You better get a move on or you'll miss your plane," John said.

"No way. I've got everything organized. All I have to do is brush my teeth, put on my makeup, and get dressed."

"You know, honey, you've got it made. When I die, I want to come back as a Los Altos housewife."

I laughed and threw my pillow at him.

We arrived at San Jose Airport a little early.

"I'll check your luggage," said John. "Why don't you wait over there where you can see Sharon when she arrives?"

I no sooner sat down than Sharon rushed in holding luggage in one hand and dragging golf clubs with the other.

"Where's Bob?" I asked.

"Oh, he just dropped me off at the entrance."

As she waited in line to check in her luggage, John whispered to me, "I would never do that to you."

"Do what?"

"Just drop you off like that. You never know if you'll see your loved one again."

"God, John, what a morbid thing to say. Nothing bad is going to happen."

John walked with us to the waiting area and sat with us until boarding time. He gave me a big kiss and hug.

"Bye, sweetie," I said. "I'll see you in four days. I'll call you when I arrive at Dee's place so you'll know I arrived safely. I love you."

We found our seats on the plane, strapped ourselves in, and chatted as if we hadn't seen each other in years. Sharon told me that Gerry and her husband, Gary, had been at the condo for a week, and he would be leaving that day. Dee was flying in from the East and would land in Palm Springs about the same time as we did.

A voice announced, "We will be landing in about five minutes."

"Here we are," I said, "safe and sound."

We walked down the plane steps and into the airport. As we picked up our luggage, Sharon said, "I see Gerry waiting for us in the car."

"Here comes Dee," I said. "Perfect timing."

Gerry opened the trunk for us and we stacked our luggage and golf clubs inside. I opened the back door and slid in next to Sharon.

"Gee, Gerry," I said, "this is a nice car."

"I know. I rented this new Oldsmobile, and it has

everything in it. It was fun driving from Los Gatos to Palm Springs."

All were seated and anxious to go when Gerry said, "Before I move the car, everyone has to buckle up. If I should get stopped, I could be fined if we don't have our seat belts fastened."

"You're the boss, Gerry," I said.

We buckled up. It was so hot outside that it was nice to be in a car with air conditioning.

When we arrived at the condo, Gary greeted us and carried our luggage inside. I couldn't wait to get into my swimsuit and jump into the pool. Sharon and Dee had the same idea.

"Are you going to join us, Gerry?" I asked.

"No, I'm going to drive Gary to the airport."

The three of us had the pool to ourselves.

"What a life!" I thought. "Being a Los Altos housewife is great."

After a few hours of swimming, sunning, and talking, Dee wanted to play tennis.

"It's the perfect time of day to play," she said. "The sun is going down, and we can play under the lights."

Gerry returned from the airport. We changed into tennis clothes, went to the courts, and warmed up for about ten minutes.

Gerry won the toss and elected to serve. I played poorly the first set. When it was over, we switched partners. Although I should have been warmed up by then, I continued to play badly. My feet felt heavy, and I wasn't moving well. The harder I tried the worse I did. I thought I was tired because it was late and I hadn't eaten much that day. Just one more set and then we could have dinner.

It was 8:30-8:45 when we finally sat down for dinner. Gerry had prepared a lovely chicken dinner for us. The next night would be my turn to be chef. Although I was hungry, I couldn't finish dinner. I felt strange; I didn't know why. Gerry cleared the table. Sharon asked if anyone would like to play bridge.

"I'd love to, but I'm not feeling well," I said. "I think I had too much sun."

I wanted to call John and tell him that we had landed safely. "May I use the phone to call John?"

"I don't think you'll be able to, Bev," Gerry said. "I meant to tell Dee this afternoon that the phone isn't working."

"I'll get someone to work on it tomorrow," replied Dee.

Not having a phone bothered me. I felt cut off from the world. I was disappointed; I wanted John to know we arrived safely.

I was thinking, "I don't know what's wrong with me. Why do I feel so strange? Maybe I'm overly tired. I'll go to bed early and get a good night's sleep. That'll do the trick."

So I said, "Good night, everyone, I'm going to hit the hay. See you in the morning."

Sharon stood and responded, "That sounds like a good idea. I'll join you."

Sharon and I shared a bedroom. She picked the bed by the window, so I took the one by the air conditioner. After we prepared for bed, we said "Good night," and Sharon turned off the light. The air was still very warm. The air conditioner clicked on and off and kept me awake. When it stayed off too long, the room was hot, and when it was on too long, it was cold. I could hear Sharon tossing and turning. What a strange night. First, I was hungry and could barely eat and then I was tired and couldn't sleep.

Sharon got up.

"Having trouble sleeping?" I asked.

"Yes, I need a drink of water."

"Me, too."

"I'll bring one back for you," she said.

When Sharon returned, we sipped our water and talked for awhile.

"I guess we should try to get some sleep," I said. "We have a big day tomorrow. I wish I had another blanket. The air conditioner is blowing on me."

Sharon replied, "I'm hot over here. Do you want to swap beds?"

"Sounds great."

I was more comfortable by the window. The next I knew, the alarm went off. I felt I had just fallen asleep. We were slow getting up. As I got out of bed, I still didn't feel well. I didn't know what was wrong. I wasn't feverish and had no headache or stomach ache. My body felt heavy. I thought about staying home and resting. I didn't feel like playing golf. I sat down and ate my bowl of cereal, hoping that it would make me feel better. It didn't help much, but I decided to play anyway. I hoped playing golf would distract me from the way I felt.

The four of us drove to the golf course, removed our clubs from the car, checked in at the clubhouse, and went to the first tee. Once I started to play, I forgot how badly I had been feeling. When we had finally finished the round, we headed for the clubhouse.

"I can't believe we made it, playing eighteen holes in this heat," said Gerry.

"Let's get inside and add up our scores," panted Dee.

"Does anyone have a calculator I can borrow?" I joked.

The clubhouse was cool. We found an empty table and sat down. The waiter took our order. We had two rounds of drinks: Gerry had beer, Dee had vodka collins, and Sharon and I had 7-up. We finally added our scores. Gerry had the best score. She was the only one to break 100.

"Wow," said Gerry, "I can't wait to tell Gary. Can I keep the scorecard? I think I'll frame it."

It was about 2:30 when we decided to leave.

"Where are we going to play tomorrow?" asked Sharon.

Dee mentioned the name of another golf course and said we could call for a starting time when we got home.

"No, we can't," said Gerry. "Remember, the phone isn't working."

Sharon suggested that we drive to the golf course, sign up for the next day, and then head for home.

"Sounds good to me," I said.

Gerry turned to me and asked, "Would you mind driving? I don't think I should drive after two beers."

"I'd rather not, Gerry. I'm uncomfortable driving in an unfamiliar area."

Sharon offered to drive. We left the clubhouse and headed for the car. Sharon opened the trunk and we put our clubs inside. I opened the door and slid into the seat next to Sharon. Dee asked if I would mind sitting in the back, because she gets car sick.

"That's fine with me," I said.

I moved to the right back seat next to Gerry.

"Remember to buckle up," cautioned Gerry.

As Sharon drove, Gerry and I talked about our golf game. We drove down Bob Hope Drive, a two-lane road.

Then ... the accident.

35

7

At Home

John was at home, enjoying his first day of sabbatical leave. When the phone rang about 4:30 that afternoon, he debated whether to answer it. He was tired and didn't want to talk. Instinctively, he thought he should answer it.

"Hello."

The voice on the phone asked to speak to John Differding.

"This is he."

"This is the Highway Patrol calling. Your wife has been in a traffic accident."

John's heart pounded.

"How is she?"

"She is being taken by ambulance to Desert Hospital in Palm Springs. I'll give you the phone number. They will be able to tell you her condition."

John took down the number, said "Thank you," and hung up. He called Desert Hospital and asked for Emergency.

"Can you tell me if Beverly Differding has been admitted? The Highway Patrol told me that she would be brought to your hospital."

"Just a moment." And then, "I'm sorry. No one by that name has been admitted to the Emergency Room. When were you notified?"

"Just a few minutes ago."

"She will probably be arriving soon."

"If you don't mind, I would like to stay on the line until she arrives."

"All right."

As John waited, he imagined the injuries that I might have.

In several minutes, a voice said, "She is being brought in now."

"How is she?"

"Just a moment." And then, "She's in critical condition. We probably will be taking her to surgery."

"Please tell her that I am on my way there, and please come back and tell me that she has received the message."

"Yes, sir, I will."

Someone was calling my name, "Mrs. Differding, Mrs. Differding."

Everything was dark. I couldn't see anything. I could hear footsteps, moving quickly, almost running. I could feel the gurney moving and hear its wheels. I was cold. I didn't feel pain, just numbness. Why were they hurrying?

"Mrs. Differding," repeated an anxious voice, "Your husband is on the phone. He wants you to know that he is on his way. Can you hear me?"

I managed a soft "Yes, thank you." Then I lost consciousness.

"Mr. Differding, she heard me."

"Thank you."

John felt some relief as he hung up.

"At least she's conscious," he thought.

He immediately called to schedule the earliest flight to Palm Springs. There were no through flights, either from San Jose or San Francisco Airport. There was a flight from San

Francisco to Ontario with a 45 minute wait before a second flight continued to Palm Springs. The San Francisco flight was leaving in less than an hour. There wasn't time to pack luggage. He grabbed his toilet kit, wallet, and keys and hastily drove to S.F. Airport. He parked the car and ran to the ticket office, relieved to find that he was in time to board the plane. However, the takeoff was delayed for 45 minutes, and by the time the plane arrived in Ontario, the connecting flight had already left for Palm Springs. The next flight to Palm Springs didn't leave for two hours.

While John waited in Ontario, he called his older daughter to tell her what had happened. He said he would call her from Palm Springs as soon as he knew what the situation was.

The flight to Palm Springs was late, so John rented a car and drove to Palm Springs. He arrived at the hospital just before midnight. The main entrance was dark and it was several minutes before he found the Emergency Entrance. I was still in the Recovery Room, so John went to the Admissions Office to fill out forms for hospitalization and insurance coverage. When John returned to the Intensive Care Unit, my bed was still empty.

8

Emergency Surgery

From the nurses John learned that I had been severely injured by a lap belt, with extensive abdominal hemorrhage and paraplegia. When I was admitted, my temperature had been 95, pulse 40, respirations 28 and shallow, and no palpable blood pressure. (Normally, my temperature is 98, pulse 60, respirations 10, and blood pressure 100/60.) There was a brace around my neck, because of suspected neck injuries. Multiple IV's were in place. My condition was critical.

John was introduced to my doctor who told him my condition.

"She was in surgery for two hours. She had a complete transection of her abdominal muscles. There were multiple transections of her small intestines, with one piece floating free in the abdomen. There was a tear in the the soft tissue supporting the small intestine, down to the aorta, with severe arterial bleeding. We reconnected the small intestine as best we could. The first part of the large intestine had exploded, and the large intestine on the other side was disrupted. We closed off the large intestine and put in an ostomy (an opening from the intestine to the outside for drainage).

"We put in a second opening from the large intestine to the outside to decompress the remainder of the large intestine. We tied off as many bleeding sites as we could, but there is blood oozing from so many sites, that we had to leave packs in the abdominal cavity. More than 3,000 cc. of blood was removed. Three drains were placed in her flanks to prevent her abdomen from filling up. She is paraplegic and obviously has a serious spinal cord injury. She is lying on a board to prevent further damage to her spinal cord. There may be intestinal leaks that we didn't detect. Some of her bowel may not have an adequate blood supply and will die.

"We plan to take her back to surgery in 24-48 hours and re-explore her abdomen for bleeding sites, bowel leaks, and the removal of any dead bowel. She will have to remain on a board until her abdomen heals enough for us to turn her over and have her spinal cord explored. Unfortunately, the board will cause a bedsore to develop over her sacrum.

"Because of the massive hemorrhage, we were unable to explore her kidneys and ureters, and they may well have been damaged. A catheter in her bladder has produced some urine, so at least one of her kidneys is still functioning.

"She has a three-inch laceration across her chin which has been closed with metal clips. She has multiple lacerations of the hands and one on her right leg which we have not sutured. She has an arterial catheter in her right wrist so that we can monitor her blood pressure, pulse, and heart rate. There are leads attached to her chest so that we can view her electrocardiogram.

"She has a venous catheter in the right subclavian vein beneath the collarbone, so we can measure venous pressure and administer fluids and medications.

"There is a nasogastric tube in place, so that we can continuously remove fluid from her stomach. It is important that almost nothing pass into her intestine while it is healing.

"She has a tube from her mouth into her windpipe so that we can give her artificial respiration. She has been sedated so she will rest. Because of the endotracheal tube, she will not be able to speak to you."

Desert Hospital is a regional trauma center. Their intensive care units are modern and well-planned, with each having a central nursing station and surrounding patient rooms. The circular arrangement allows nurses to see into each room and observe the monitors at the same time. The monitors show heart rate, blood pressure, and an electrocardiogram simultaneously. The nurses are well-trained, efficient and friendly.

I was barely aware of nurses continually coming into my room to check the monitors and replace the containers of fluids that were slowly dripping into my intravenous catheter. When the containers were low, a buzzer went off to alert the nurses that they needed to be removed or replaced. The sound often woke me up. Blood was frequently drawn from my intra-arterial line. The amount of bloody fluid coming from my drains and my urine output were measured, so the fluid could be replaced.

I was vaguely aware that John was with me most of the time, sitting in a chair beside my bed. My vision was blurred. I couldn't tell the time on the large clock on the wall. Sometimes I couldn't tell who was in the room.

My hands were restrained so that I wouldn't dislodge any of the tubes or catheters. The tubes in my nose and throat were uncomfortable. It was aggravating not to be able to reach them. The board beneath me was uncomfortable. When the pain was severe, I rolled my head from side to side, and I could feel the board.

The next day, X-rays showed that I had fractures of 3rd

and 4th lumbar vertebrae, with considerable displacement of some fragments. My back was unstable there. I had disc herniation of my lumbosacral joint. I had some fluid in my chest cavities. There was a moderate amount of fluid and a small amount of air in my abdomen. A curious finding was the presence of one of my earrings embedded in the skin of my back. The impact had been so great that it had dislodged the earring from my pierced ear.

About 36 hours after my first surgery, I was taken to the operating room for a second look. Fortunately, there was no dead bowel. The suture lines were intact with no apparent leaks. The packs were removed and there was no new bleeding. Only the upper part of the abdominal wall could be reconstructed. The muscles in the lower part of the wall had been crushed. I had metal staples from my breastbone to my pubic bone.

The next day my hemoglobin dropped to 5.1. (It's usually about 13.0.) Transfusions were started. I was relieved to have the tube from my mouth into my windpipe removed. My nose, throat, and mouth were continually dry. I could only suck on ice chips or have a damp sponge on my lips. When I learned I could occasionally have a popsicle, I constantly wanted one. I don't know how long I had been in the hospital when I heard John's voice.

"Hi, Babe, I'm here."

"Oh, John," I tried to say.

"It's all right, honey. Try not to talk. You need to save your strength. The doctors want you to lie still. They haven't had a chance to do your back surgery. Your abdominal injuries had to be taken care of first."

My chin hurt. I strained to touch it and felt something like a zipper along the bottom of my chin.

"Hon, leave that alone. You had a deep cut on your chin and the doctors closed it with surgical staples."

I tried to pull them off. John gently put my arm down.

"It'll be fine, honey. Leave it alone so it can heal."

I wasn't sure how much damage I had suffered, but I knew I was in bad shape. Many thoughts ran through my mind. I didn't want to be a burden to my loved ones. I couldn't do that. I felt John's warm hand holding mine. I slowly turned my head toward him.

"John, I want you to know that you are free to leave me. I will understand."

He squeezed my hand and said, "I'd like to hang around if you don't mind."

I smiled as tears ran down my cheeks.

"I love you," I sighed and closed my eyes.

9

Deciding to Live

Each time I awoke, John was there, holding my hand. The pain grew stronger. I had never experienced anything so terrible. At times I sobbed uncontrollably and rolled my head from side to side. I felt as if I could only move my head.

I was getting large doses of pain medication every four hours. I thank God that John was there to make sure the nurses gave me my shots on time. I was weak. I looked at John. His face was pale and tired. I could tell he was suffering with me.

"John, are Gerry and Sharon dead?"

"Yes, they both died in the accident."

"I thought so. How is Dee?"

"She had a head injury with some weakness of the right side and had several fractured ribs. Ten days in the hospital and she will be able to go home."

"I'm angry with Sharon and Gerry for leaving me behind. They're in a beautiful place, and I'm still here with so much pain. Why didn't He take me too?"

I began to cry.

"Oh, John, I hurt so badly, I don't know if I want to go on."

"Sure you do, Babe. Hang in there. I'll be here to help you."

I was thinking, "Please don't ask me to stay. I don't know if I want to. The pain is too great. You don't understand. I don't want to let you down."

I let out a big sigh.

44

"John, I have something to ask of you."

"Sure, hon, what is it?"

"I want your permission to let me choose to die if I wish to."

I know it sounds strange, but I knew I could choose to live or die. I was thinking of letting go. I could tell I had surprised him. He hesitated for a moment.

"I'll do whatever you want, but I want you to know that I love you very much, and I hope that you choose to live."

My son Gary, his wife Stephanie, and my parents arrived. They were trying to be brave.

I was lucky to have such a loving and caring family.

John was at my side, watching the monitors and not allowing anyone to stay very long. When Mom and Dad came in, I asked them, too, for their permission to let me choose to live or die. Their eyes filled with tears. They didn't want to agree; they didn't want to lose me. It was very difficult for them, but they finally agreed. My younger son, Ken, drove in from Tempe, Arizona where he was attending college. When he looked at me, I could see the shock in his eyes. He held my hand with both of his and smiled as tears ran down his face.

"Hi, mom."

"Hi, sweetheart," I whispered.

There was silence as we looked at each other. Our thoughts took the place of words. I finally asked about school. I was trying to find the courage to ask him to let me die if I chose. Fatigue was setting in. My voice was weak. It was time to ask. I watched his face as I began my request. He was trying hard to be brave. He lowered his head and looked at the floor. His shoulders shook. As he lifted his head, tears streamed down his face.

"I'll do anything you want, Mom."

His face was wrenched with pain. He began to sob uncontrollably as he spoke.

"I love you so much, Mom. I don't want you to die."

At that moment I realized how much he needed me. He was alone. His pain hurt me more than the sharp pains surging through my body. I couldn't leave him.

I put my hand to his face.

"It's all right, Kenny. I'm not going to leave you."

I had made my decision. I would fight for my life. It would be a difficult battle. I needed a lot of help. At that moment, I remembered the Bible saying: Ask and you shall receive.

I closed my eyes and whispered, "Dear Lord, I'm asking. Please help me. Heal my body."

10

Back Surgery

A neurosurgeon examined me in preparation for my back surgery. Urine was leaking through my right flank drain, indicating that I had an injury to my kidney or ureter. He said that I should have back surgery before I was transferred to a hospital in the Bay Area.

One physician had suggested that I have an MRI (magnetic resonance imaging) scan. John reminded him that I should not have one because of the many metal staples in my body. They could be pulled out by the strong magnet and would interfere with the pictures. Thank God John was with me.

The next day, a urologist came to evaluate the urine drainage and determine whether that problem should be treated prior to my back surgery. The amount of urine passing through the drain was about the same as was coming from my bladder, indicating that most or all of my right kidney output was draining out my side. The urologist felt that I had transection of the ureter on that side. He recommended that I have back surgery first. Although John and I wanted me to return to Stanford Medical Center for further surgery, both neurosurgeons felt that my condition was too critical for transfer. My intestine was still not working. Fortunately, two days before my scheduled back surgery, my intestines began to function. The nasogastric tube, that continually hurt my nose and irritated my throat, could be removed. For a week I had had nothing by mouth, except for ice chips and an occasional popsicle. My chin staples were taken out. The drains in my left side were removed. There was still urine coming from the drain in my right side, and it couldn't be removed until I had kidney surgery.

Friends at home had donated six units of blood for me. My friend Nancy and her husband flew to Palm Springs with the units in an ice pack, so the blood would be available for my back surgery. John talked with them in the hospital lobby, but I didn't have a chance to see them.

The day before my back surgery, one neurosurgeon recommended that I have a lumbar myelogram and another felt it wasn't necessary. John argued that if it wasn't clearly necessary, it shouldn't be done. The chief neurosurgeon insisted, so John reluctantly signed the consent form. The myelogram revealed an extensive spinal fluid leak in the region of the 3rd and 4th lumbar vertebrae.

The next day I was taken to the operating room. After the skin was incised, spinal fluid was evident in the wound. There was partial transection and extensive bruising of the lumbar paraspinal muscles. There was an extension of the wound into the abdominal cavity. When the spinal canal was exposed, a complete transection of the nerves at the end of the spinal cord was seen. The nerves lying free in the wound were the distal ends. The proximal ends were retracted upward beyond the level of exposure and could not be seen. The spinal fluid leak was repaired. Two Harrington rods were placed between the 1st and 5th lumbar vertebrae to stabilize my spine. Bone for a bone graft was obtained from the iliac crest. I was taken to the recovery room in critical condition.

After I had been returned to my room, I was in great pain. I remember when they removed me from the wooden stretcher. They carefully slipped me onto the bed, and I was able to feel the softness of the mattress and smell the clean sheets. I sighed with relief.

The neurosurgeon came to tell me about the surgery. He said that since he had not been able to repair my completely transected spinal cord, I would not be able to walk again.

I knew that wasn't true. I can't explain it. I just knew. Very calmly, I told him he was wrong.

He was shocked that I contradicted him.

I sensed his uneasiness as he patted my hand and said, "I hope so, my dear, I hope so."

I was at peace and not the least bit upset that he didn't believe what I had said.

The doctor took John aside and told him, "You'd better tell your wife where she is. She has to be realistic. If you don't make her realize that she is not going to walk again, she will have serious emotional problems later on."

After the back surgery my pain was greater. At times I thought the pain would kill me. I was given more medication to try to control it.

One afternoon I thought I was looking through a big window and could see Mom and Dad standing in front of the hospital door. I was very upset because they were afraid to come in to see me. I started yelling at them to come in. John was trying to calm me.

"Honey, there isn't a large window in your room. Your parents aren't here."

"Yes, they are! Can't you see them?"

I finally screamed, "Get the hell in here!"

John kept trying to convince me that they weren't there.

"Babe, you're hallucinating. It's all right."

John explained that sometimes medications can cause

you to see or hear things that seem real but aren't. It was difficult to believe him. I know what I saw.

John was with me almost all of the time. He slept at a motel just a short walk from the hospital. He came about four in the morning and stayed until seven when the new shift of nurses arrived. Then he went to the hospital cafeteria for breakfast. The only time he wasn't with me was when he ate and slept.

One evening a nurse came in to remove the nasogastric tube.

"Thank God," I thought. "How I hate that tube."

"All right," she said, "try not to move as I'm pulling it out."

It seemed to take forever. It felt like the tube extended down into my toes. I was so happy to have it removed. My throat was sore, but at least the tube was out.

Several hours passed, and I thought all was going well. The nurse came back to check me. She was concerned about my stomach and left the room to return shortly with another nurse.

"Now what?" I thought.

"I'm sorry, Mrs. Differding, but your stomach is swelling. We'll have to put another tube into your nose."

"Oh, no!" I cried, "not again."

The nurses opened a new package with a thin tube in it. Lubricant was put on the end of the tube, and they began inserting the tube into my nose. I felt it passing through my nose and into my throat. Suddenly, I was choking. I could feel my heart pounding. I couldn't breathe. My eyes bulged. I tried to tell them I couldn't breathe, but I couldn't make a sound. They kept pushing the tube in.

John realized what was happening and yelled, "Take it out! She can't breathe. It's going down the wrong way."

When they removed it, I began to cry.

"Please, John, don't let them do this to me."

The nurse apologized. She told John that this was the first time this had happened to her. I was sobbing and pleading with John not to let them force that tube into my nose. John was upset and felt badly for me. They asked him to leave the room until they could replace the tube. Although I was crying and nearly hysterical, they were finally able to get the tube into my stomach. Several days later, it was finally removed. Generally, the nursing staff was excellent, but one morning a nurse came into my room that I didn't recognize.

"Good morning," she said.

"Hi," I replied. "I don't remember seeing you before. Are you new?"

"I'm filling in for Laurie. What brought you to us?"

"I was in a car accident, hit head-on by a drunk driver."

She said she was a treated alcoholic and told me extensively of her personal difficulties. I was uncomfortable having her there. As she talked, she began to raise the head of my bed.

"Stop," I said. "My doctor wants me to lay flat."

"Oh, this little bit won't hurt anything."

I knew she was wrong, but I was too tired to argue. I was relieved when she finally left but concerned about the upright position she left me in. I hoped John or my doctor would come soon.

When the neurosurgeon came in and found the head of my bed elevated, he was furious. That position put strain on my recently operated back. He lowered the head of the bed and disconnected the bed so it couldn't be moved.

"I want to know the name of the nurse who didn't read

the chart," the doctor said.

John told me the doctor gave the nurse a stern lecture and filed an incident report. I didn't see that nurse again.

Three days after my back surgery, I was still in great pain. There were times that I wished I would die. A TENS (transcutaneous electrical nerve stimulator) unit was applied to my midback. It works by causing a slight shock that distracts the brain from the severe pain arising below it. Over the next two days, the TENS unit markedly decreased the amount of pain medication that I had to take.

My intestine wasn't working, and the detested nasogastric tube was still in place. Some Radiology personnel came to do an intravenous pyelogram, which showed that I had a disrupted right ureter near the kidney.

A respiratory therapist came every day to see that I coughed and took deep breaths to expand my lungs. These exercises help prevent pneumonia. It took much effort, but I seemed to improve each time.

It was painful to be turned to have my back examined, but there was still some drainage from my back surgery, and the bedsore over my sacrum had to be cleaned and covered. I often had wraps around my legs up to the mid-thighs to prevent swelling and braces on my feet to prevent foot drop. Other times I had soft boots on my feet to prevent pressure sores.

11

Some Good Things

The happiest time of each day was when the mail arrived. I was amazed at all the cards and letters I received. John opened them and slowly read them to me, so the only good part of my day would be prolonged. It gave me strength and encouragement to know that so many friends were thinking of me. When it seemed like forever before I would get my next pain medication, John would re-read some of the letters to me.

I received many beautiful flowers, but hospital rules didn't allow them in the Intensive Care Unit. We gave some to patients that the nurses said had received no flowers or letters. John gave one of the prettiest bouquets to a nurse who had been especially kind to me.

A priest came to see me several times, and I greatly appreciated his blessings. Every day, John called friends and relatives to inform them of my progress, and they spread the word to many others.

Finally, five days after my back surgery, my intestine began to function, and I had the nasogastric tube removed. The next day I started a soft diet, and I felt much better. The arterial line in my right wrist was removed. We could now start planning for my transfer to Stanford Medical Center.

Palm Springs was too far from Stanford for me to be transferred by helicopter, so I was to be flown by Lear jet to Moffett Field and then by helicopter to Stanford Medical Center.

John had trouble arranging for a hospital bed for me at Stanford in the Community Service Intensive Care Unit. The head of the unit was on vacation and no one else was willing to arrange for my transfer. Fortunately, a physician friend of John's knew the head of the Stanford Service Intensive Care Unit and was able to arrange for a bed for me. At last, it looked like I would be leaving for the Bay Area.

The day before I was to leave, the intravenous medications were stopped. I was excited to see the nurses pack my belongings. All of my abdominal staples were removed except for a small area below the navel. The remaining staples were left in place because there was no underlying muscular support. During the trip to Stanford I was to have nothing by mouth and no medications.

The morning I was to leave, a doctor and his assistant arrived from Stanford. He wanted X-rays to check the placement of the intravenous catheter beneath my collarbone, a procedure that the nursing staff had not anticipated. After some time, a radiology team came to take portable films. The X-rays appeared to show a partial collapse of the lower lobe of my left lung. The central venous catheter tip extended into the upper right atrium of my heart. The Stanford doctor gave me an anesthetic around the intravenous catheter site, so that he could partly withdraw the catheter and leave the tip in a safer place. After that was done, I was ready to go. My doctors came to say good-bye. My abdominal surgeon called me his miracle lady and wished me luck. Several nurses gathered around with tears in their eyes and wished me well. We had become so attached. I said a tearful goodbye.

54

I was placed on a gurney and lifted into an ambulance. John stayed with me. The ambulance drove slowly, but I could feel every bump. When we arrived at the airfield, I saw the small plane that was to fly me to the Bay Area. The door was small and it was difficult to get the stretcher with me on it through the door. There was little room inside and John sat in the rear of the plane at my head. I was very tense about being in such a claustrophobic situation.

The plane took off in moderate winds. Until we were out of the valley, we were blown about irregularly, like being on the ocean in a small ship. The stretcher was uncomfortable, and the space was too small for me to move my arms. After an hour and a half, we landed at Moffett Field in Mountain View. We had planned to go by helicopter from there to Stanford, but Secretary Schultz was visiting Stanford, and the authorities would not permit a flight from Moffett Field to Stanford. I was put in an ambulance and driven to Stanford. Bayshore Freeway was in poor condition, and the repeated jarring hurt me badly. I was in great pain, very upset, and exhausted.

Stanford
Medical Center

12

Intensive Care Ward

By early afternoon I finally arrived at the Stanford Emergency entrance. The doors automatically opened and the paramedics wheeled me into the hospital. I recognized the distinctive odor that hospitals have. I wanted my journey to end. Every movement hurt my back, and I was exhausted.

My daughter-in-law, Stephanie, who worked in pediatrics at Stanford, had arranged in advance for my admission. What a relief not to have to answer 101 questions at the Admissions Desk before I could go to my room.

So, without delay, I was taken to the Intensive Care ward. I had been assigned a room at the end of the hall. I was wheeled into a two-patient room so small that my gurney could barely fit between the bed and the sink. Compared to the excellent intensive care unit in Desert Hospital, everything here seemed drab, cramped, and old. But I was happy to be close to home, family, and friends.

Once I was settled, I looked around. On my left, three feet from the bed, was a sink and cabinets. On the other side, two feet from my bed, was an ugly plastic curtain that partly divided the room in two. I couldn't see the patient next to me, but I knew someone was there; I could hear the swooshing sound of a respirator.

John was by my side, holding my hand. He told me he had to get a ride home so he could check on the dogs and the house, pick up his car, and see how things were at work. He thought I would be all right now that I was at Stanford. He gave me a kiss and told me he would be back later. I hated to see him leave. He had been almost constantly at my side since the accident, and I felt lost without him.

I hadn't had food or pain medication since I left Palm Springs. The pain was agonizing. I called for the nurse.

"I need something for my pain."

"I'm sorry. I have to check with your doctor first."

"What about something to eat? I haven't eaten all day."

"I'll call the kitchen for you."

My friend, Dottie, who does volunteer work at Stanford, came in to greet me, "Welcome home, Bevie."

She leaned over and gave me a peck on the cheek. She held my face in her hands and had tears in her eyes.

"All your friends have been waiting for the day that you would come home to us."

"Oh, Dottie, I'm so glad to see you."

We both cried.

"Bevie, I'm not supposed to stay long. I'll come back tomorrow and check in on you."

She left and I continued to cry.

Stephanie arrived.

"Hi, mom. How are you doing?"

"Hi, sweetie. I'm surviving."

"I called Gary to let him know that you're at Stanford."

"Thanks, Steph."

"You're not supposed to have visitors today, but I'm working here till five and I'll drop by before I go home. Gary will come to see you tomorrow night. I love you."

"I love you, too, Steph. Tell Gary I miss him."

She kissed me good-bye and left.

I missed company. The pain was difficult to tolerate, but at least, without medication, I was very alert.

What a choice, either alert and much pain, or less pain and goofy. The pain was becoming intolerable.

I knew I wouldn't get anything for my pain until the doctor arrived. Heaven only knew when that would be. I thought I could at least get something to eat, so I called for the nurse.

"When will I get some food?"

"Oh, I haven't had time to call for you."

"That's great," I thought. "It's almost dinner time."

"Will I get any dinner?"

"It's too late to fill out a menu for you, but the snack lady will be around after dinner."

Just what I needed, an incompetent nurse. She couldn't care less that I was in pain and hungry. I thought the patients who needed the most care would be assigned the best nurses, but that often wasn't true. I knew my first impression could be wrong, but I couldn't overcome my dislike for this nurse.

A resident came in to talk to me. He had read my summary from Desert Hospital and asked how I was doing.

"I want to move out of intensive care."

"Why?"

"I'm not sick enough to be here. There's probably someone who needs this bed more than I do. This curtain smells. I hate the smell of plastic."

He picked up his clipboard and took notes.

"How long have you disliked the smell of plastic?"

I thought, "What a strange question." and replied, "Many people don't like the smell of plastic and certainly wouldn't want to sleep next to it."

He continued to question me about things that had nothing to do with my injuries or about moving out of intensive care.

He finally put his clipboard and pen down.

"I think you should talk to a psychiatrist. You're preoccupied with the smell of plastic."

I yelled, "I what?!"

"I think you need to stay where you are. You're a very sick woman mentally."

With that, he turned around and walked out of the room. I began to cry.

"My God, he thinks I'm crazy. He's not going to let me leave this horrible room."

It was soon dinner time. I was alone except for the patient on the other side of the curtain and my nurse, Miss Wonderful. My leg pain was fierce, and my stomach was empty. I couldn't do anything except wait for John to return. I closed my eyes and tried to sleep.

As I lay there, I heard faint voices, "Beverly. Beverly. We're here to help you."

I opened my eyes and looked around the room. I couldn't tell where the voices were coming from. They kept repeating that they were there to heal me. The voices were so clear, I was surprised that the nurse didn't pay attention. She was reading something. I listened intently. I could hear the respirator. I knew I wasn't dreaming. Finally, the voices stopped. I didn't know what to think. Perhaps I was getting withdrawal symptoms from not having any pain medication. Then I realized that it must be my spirit healers telling me they were taking care of me. I wasn't sure. I wanted to ask John if he thought withdrawal could make me hear voices.

I was relieved when John finally arrived. I told him that I

hadn't had any medication or food. He could see I was in great pain and became very angry. He had assumed that since I was now in Stanford, that everything would be going well.

As he turned to the nurse, I could tell he was trying to stay calm.

"My wife needs medication for her pain, NOW!"

"I'm sorry," said the nurse. "I haven't received any orders from her doctor."

She started to tell John the hospital rules, and John interrupted, "I know what the rules are. I'm a physician on the staff here. So kindly locate the doctor and ask him to write an order for my wife's medication. This should have been taken care of when she first arrived."

The nurse showed no emotion. She picked up the phone to locate my doctor.

John asked if a doctor had been to see me. When I told him that a resident had told me that I was mentally disturbed, he exploded.

"God damn it!" he said. "What's his name? I don't want him anywhere near you. He's some smart ass just out of school who has no idea what you've been through."

"Honey," I said, "Don't get upset. He isn't worth it. I don't care if he thinks I'm crazy."

"I care. He has no right talking to any patient that way. He'll hear from me."

I tried to calm him down. He was already stressed and exhausted from spending so much time with me in the hospital. I worried about him.

"I'll be right back," he said, and he was out the door.

I know John. If John finds him, that resident is in for a big shock.

John soon returned.

"I couldn't find the resident, so I called the head of intensive care to tell him what had happened. From now on, you won't have that resident as one of your doctors."

I told John about my spirit healers, and what they said to me.

"Do you think it's the drugs that made me hear them?"

"No, Babe. You haven't had any drugs since we left Palm Springs."

"Maybe I'm going crazy?"

"Honey, I believe you. I know someone is looking out for you. It's a miracle you're still here."

The nurse returned with a syringe. She had talked to my doctor who had ordered some pain medication. She came to the side of the bed and asked, "Where should I give you your shot?"

John and I looked at each other, wondering if we had heard correctly.

"They have been giving her shots in the thighs," said John.

I wasn't sure just where I had been getting shots, since I hadn't been able to feel them. I was in for a big surprise. The nurse gave my thigh a quick wipe with a square of alcohol-soaked cotton. Then she stuck the needle into my thigh and injected the solution. I let out a yell. John was obviously irritated. She pulled out the needle, looked at John in bewilderment, and left the room.

"She didn't pull back on the syringe to be sure she wasn't in a blood vessel," criticized John.

My thigh hurt and a lump was forming at the injection site. John came over to the other side of the bed to rub my thigh.

Then he went down to the cafeteria and came back

with some pastry for me. He didn't stay long. He promised to return early in the morning.

I had a hard time sleeping. The respirator noise was bothersome, and sometimes I heard choking sounds coming from the patient in the next bed. I wondered who was on the other side of the smelly curtain. The smell nauseated me.

In the morning when I awoke, I was still tired. I looked around to see that nothing had changed. I hated the room's irritating sounds and smells. I knew I didn't need to be in intensive care.

A male nurse came in to talk to the patient next to me. When the nurse finished, he introduced himself to me. He was my nurse for the day.

"I'll be taking care of you till three o'clock today."

He was pleasant, knowledgeable, interested in how I was doing, and a welcome replacement. I was relieved to have a friendly nurse. With him I felt safe. He checked my chart and went over it with me.

"I heard you didn't have anything to eat yesterday."

"That's right. Do you think I'll get breakfast this morning?"

"I know you will. I've called the kitchen and ordered your breakfast. I wasn't sure what you like, so I ordered a little of everything."

"You're an angel," I said with a smile. "I'm so hungry I would eat anything."

John arrived as my breakfast tray was delivered. The nurse, bless his heart, had ordered enough food for three people. Everything on the tray looked good. I thought I could eat everything. But after I finished my egg and a few bites of toast, I felt full. My stomach must have shrunk. I asked John to help me finish the breakfast.

A little after nine, a group of doctors making rounds came in. It was the first time I'd seen my doctor. There were numerous questions, and John helped answer them. Several times I mentioned that I thought I didn't belong in intensive care and wanted to move. No one seemed to listen to me.

When the doctors left, I asked John if I could be moved.

"We'll have to wait and see. I don't know if they have a vacant room for you."

"Don't you agree that I don't belong here?"

"I'm not sure, Babe. Let's leave it up to the doctor."

John then left to take care of some of the things that had been neglected since the accident. He assured me he would be back by noon.

Two women came to visit the patient next to me. They smiled at me and said, "Good morning." They introduced themselves as the patient's mother and grandmother. With only room for one chair in the room, the mother stood while the grandmother sat. The mother asked what had happened to me, so I told her my story. She told me that her sixteen-year-old son, my roommate, had been seriously injured in a motorcycle accident and had been in intensive care for eleven months. This was to be a big day for him, for they were taking him off the respirator.

Several doctors came in to disconnect him from the respirator and remove the tube from his throat. With the curtain between us, I couldn't see anything, but I could hear gagging and moaning.

I was happy to hear the doctor say, "How's that? I'll bet you're glad to be rid of that thing."

I heard his mom ask, "Will he be able to speak now?"

"Yes, but his throat will be sore for awhile. It would be

a good idea not to have him talk too much

When we heard, "Hi, mom," everyone ch

His mom told me her son would be moved t
room in a few days. I was happy for them.

I spent the rest of the day waiting to see if I woula
transferred out of intensive care. The nurse didn't know,
and my doctor didn't come by again. John tried to find out
if there was an open bed in intermediate care. Stephanie
came in with good news. She had been able to arrange for
a private room for me downstairs in intermediate care.

13

Intermediate Care Ward

I was wheeled to my new room late that afternoon.

I continued to have severe pain and often asked for pain
medication. Although the drugs deadened the pain, they
also dulled my perceptions and caused me to be confused
and not alert. I had a difficult time remembering what day it
was, what time it was, and when John and my parents had
come to visit me. I couldn't recall when they had said they
were coming back to visit me. I had great mood swings. At
times I had faith that I would get better, and other times I
hurt so much that I wanted to die. I was often nauseated and
didn't want my friends to see me in my present condition.

TENS(trans-cutaneous electric nerve stimulators) were
placed on my back to try to lessen my pain. They gave an
adjustable electric current to the skin above my injury. It
was uncomfortable, but better than the pain from my
injured back and legs. I had inflatable compression wraps
around my legs which intermittently increased the pressure
on my legs. Their purpose was to squeeze blood out of my
legs so that I wouldn't get clots in the veins. They were
often uncomfortably hot, and sometimes I couldn't resist
removing them. I was lying in an air bed so that there
wouldn't be pressure on my back and bedsore. I had to be
turned every two hours so that I wouldn't get other pressure sores. I had a catheter in my bladder and an ileostomy

bag. It seemed like someone was always coming to draw blood. It was very tiring and depressing.

Everything wasn't bleak. Many beautiful flowers were delivered to my room. They reminded me of all the wonderful friends I have. Each day John opened the letters and cards I received and read them to me. One gift that I especially treasured was a book about the 23rd psalm. Each day John read part of it to me. My vision was growing sharper, and John and I were relieved to find that an eye exam showed no apparent damage. The poor vision that I had had after the accident was apparently the result of a concussion.

I was continually aware that urine was still coming out of my right side and that I would have to go to surgery to have it repaired. John had talked to some of the medical staff to see who they thought was the best urologist for my surgery. He was very happy that an excellent urologist on the staff had agreed to operate on me.

Four days after admission I was taken to the operating room to have my bladder examined and to see if the urologist could pass a catheter from my bladder through the damaged right ureter to the kidney. I really hoped they would be successful, so I wouldn't have to have another surgery. The operating room was very bright. The doctor and nurses were dressed in green gowns, caps, and masks and wore rubber gloves. After they put me on the table, the doctor told me what he hoped to do. I was very anxious.

"When are you going to put me to sleep?"

"It isn't necessary for this procedure. Because of your condition, you won't feel anything."

I was thinking, "Only terror." I would rather have been

asleep. Every "hummm","darn", and "still can't reach it" made me anxious.

After what seemed a very long time, they were apparently finished.

The doctor said, "I'm sorry, Mrs. Differding. We weren't able to pass the catheter into the kidney. We will have to operate on you at a later date."

I began to cry and cried all the way back to my room. I couldn't bear going through another major surgery. The doctor was very understanding. He held my hand and tried to console me.

John talked to the doctor and then to me.

"Part of the ureter was missing. There was no way that he could repair it from below. At least it was worth the chance that you might be spared further surgery."

I was very depressed. I had stayed awake through the whole procedure and they hadn't been able to repair my ureter. It seemed like it was all for nothing.

"How soon will I have my surgery?"

"I don't know. As soon as they can schedule it, they will let us know."

Whenever I'm very upset, my pain gets worse. Over the next few days I requested pain medication frequently.

I started having weird perceptions. Some things looked as if they were moving in slow motion. Other things that I knew were close seemed far away. I was sure I saw objects or people that John assured me were not there.

I wore a red hospital bracelet that listed the drugs that had given me bad reactions, so that no one would give them to me. John suspected that I was receiving one of them. He wanted to look through my chart to see what I had been given. The head nurse refused to let him see my chart. John was furious. The doctor in charge of intermediate care, a friend of John's, asked him not to press the matter. John didn't, but he gave the doctor his opinion.

"Hospitals are so damned afraid that they are going to be sued, that it interferes with good patient care. I'm not interested in suing the hospital. I just want to know what's going on."

My days and nights were all mixed up, as I faded in and out of sleep. I was having pain most of my waking hours. I cried much of the time and wished I would die. A tennis friend of mine, who I hadn't realized was a hospital chaplain, came to visit. He repeatedly told me I had a lot to live for and that I shouldn't give up. Although I appreciated his efforts, the pain was so overwhelming that I couldn't focus on anything else. All I wanted to do was rest and be free of the constant pain.

Many of my friends wanted to visit me, but I didn't want them to see me in this condition.

14

Kidney Surgery

Two weeks after my admission, I was scheduled for surgery. John told me that the surgeon had several options, depending upon what he found at the time of surgery.

I couldn't comprehend time. I was supposed to go to surgery about two in the afternoon. An IV was put in my wrist. John told me that the surgery schedule was often late. Sure enough, John waited with me until almost seven in the evening when I was wheeled to surgery. John wanted to talk to the anesthetist before my surgery to be sure he knew about my allergies, but John never had a chance to talk to him.

When I entered the operating room, I insisted on being put to sleep. They assured me that I would be out before I could count to ten. They were right.

I woke up in the recovery room screaming with pain. The pain was terrible. A nurse repeatedly took my pulse and blood pressure. I was crying and asking for something for the pain. Even when the nurse gave me pain medication, it didn't seem to help.

Then I heard, "Hi, babe." I opened my eyes to see John in a surgical gown. He had waited outside for a long time and when I wasn't returned to my room, he decided to come into recovery. The nurses weren't happy to have him there, but a surgeon and an anesthesiologist in recovery assured the nurses that John was on the staff. I was so happy to see him.

"Oh, John, I hurt so much."

The pain was unbelievable. I couldn't stop screaming. I was very agitated. John asked the nurse what I had been given and found out that I had been given one of the pain medications that was listed on my allergy bracelet.

John was angry.

"Damn it, didn't anybody read her chart or look at her red wristband?"

Apparently, no one had done so.

John stayed with me. Just before midnight the nurse decided that I was ready to return to my room. Half an hour passed before an orderly was available to wheel me back to my room.

The next few days I was very agitated. I hit the bed with my arms. John was usually with me and kept asking me what I was doing. I didn't realize until days later that I was hallucinating and disoriented.

I was very angry with him for continually questioning me. Any idiot could see what I was doing.

"DO YOU HAVE TO KNOW EVERYTHING I DO?" I yelled at him.

One time I thought I was holding the sheet with one hand and stitching it with the other. Another time I was trying to reach a big ripe strawberry that I thought my Dad had in his hand. He kept moving it away from my lips so I couldn't reach it. I was extremely angry with him. I tried to tighten the cap on a non-existent tube. I thought I was washing my hands with soap and water. I thought I was in my Volkswagen (I hadn't had one for twenty-five years). I kept reaching for things that I couldn't grasp. I called my mother to give her a list of groceries that she should buy for me. When she asked what for, I indignantly told her that I had to prepare dinner for the family that night. I wanted to know why I had different colored tape on each of my fingers. I remember the nurse telling the doctor that I knew who I was and what day it was, but I didn't think I was in the hospital.

When Gary came, I grasped his fingers and tried to wire them together. When John asked what I was doing, I calmly said, "I'm crimping conduit." I don't know where I learned those words.

At the time all those things were real to me, and I was angry that others couldn't see what was obvious to me. According to John, I hallucinated for days. I had no sense of time. I remember thinking that it wasn't fair that my friends died quickly and I was stuck there, paralyzed and in constant pain.

I was alone late one night when I developed swelling of my abdomen with some pain. I rang for the nurse, and as often happened, they didn't respond right away. The swelling and pain were getting worse. I called John at home.

"Honey, something's wrong. My abdomen is swelling and I'm having pain."

"Did you ring for the nurse?"

"Yes, about twenty minutes ago, and no one's come."

"Okay, Babe, I'll be right there."

I kept ringing for the nurse, but there was no response.

When John arrived, my abdomen was distended and I was very concerned. John went to get the nurse.

John soon returned with a young doctor and the nurse. After they examined me, they reassured me that it was only gas in my intestine and that I wasn't bleeding from my recent surgery. I was relieved. They gave me some medication and I was soon relaxed and ready to sleep. Slowly I began to perceive things correctly. John told me that the surgeon had not been able to mobilize the kidney enough to connect it to a healthy ureter, and he had had to remove my kidney. John reassured me that I would do fine with just one healthy kidney.

I wasn't doing well. I had trouble keeping food down. I was losing weight. Skin was sagging from my arms. I had never been this thin. I was a miserable sight. I was depressed. My doctor thought a psychiatrist should see me, and John thought that might help. An enthusiastic young woman psychiatrist came to see me. I enjoyed her. She seemed to think I was doing as well as could be expected under the circumstances.

My doctor gave me a pill for nausea. I started to feel better and was able to keep more food down. My stomach had shrunk and I couldn't eat much.

One night when my family was visiting, I had a strange feeling in my jaws. The muscles were stiffening. I repeatedly tried to open and shut my mouth. I told John something was wrong. In a few minutes I couldn't move my jaw. My teeth were clenched. I was frightened, and through clenched teeth, told John to call the doctor. I began to cry.

When the doctor arrived, he calmly said, "Oh, that's a side effect of one of the drugs we've been giving you. It'll wear off in a couple of hours."

The doctor didn't think it was a big deal, but I was upset and scared. It's too bad doctors can't experience their patient's pain and fear, so they could better relate to their patients. My jaw kept tightening. My teeth were clenched so tight that I was afraid they would crack. I hated this place. I was so agitated, I was given a tranquilizer. Whatever it was put me out for several hours.

15

Looking Forward to Rehab

John told me that most of the physicians agreed that the best hospital for rehabilitation was Valley Medical Center. I wanted to go there as soon as possible. A physical therapist came to my room and said he was going to work with me daily.

"Now we're cooking," I thought. "It's about time."

The PT checked to see what I could do with my thighs, legs, and feet. I could move my thighs slightly. The knee joints could barely be bent. I had no motion in my feet.

He carefully tried to bend my knees. There was very little movement, and it hurt so much, tears came to my eyes. As I moaned, he reminded me that if I couldn't bend my knees, I wouldn't be able to sit in a wheelchair. He encouraged me to try and move my legs. I tried hard but I couldn't move them. I couldn't understand why I had so much pain in my legs and feet, when I had no sense of touch in them. After half an hour I was exhausted. It was frustrating to be so tired from accomplishing so little.

As the days passed, I wondered if the small improvement I saw was worth the effort, frustration, exhaustion, and pain.

I looked forward to meals, not because I enjoyed eating, but because my family was with me at those times. John came early in the morning and stayed through breakfast. I ordered more breakfast than I could eat so John would have something to eat. He was thin, and I worried that he wasn't eating enough.

At lunch time, my son, Ken, usually spent his lunch break with me. He helped me eat.

He would tease me by saying, "This is great, mom. I can repay you for all the times you told me I had to eat because it was good for me."

He was always in good spirits and brightened my day. He often held my hand and told me everything would be all right.

"You're going to get better, mom. If anyone can do it, you can."

At dinner time, Mom, Dad, Gary, and Stephanie came by. I enjoyed having my bed surrounded by so much love. When they left, John would come for the rest of the evening. I hated nighttime after my family left. I didn't like the dark or the silence. I feared something would happen to me, and no one would come to help. Some nights Mom and Dad stayed until two or three in the morning. Several times, Ken came and stayed late. He brought his pillow and blanket and slept in a chair next to my bed. Those nights I felt safe.

One day the doctor came in to tell me that yeast had been cultured from my bladder. I would have to have my bladder irrigated with antifungal medication until the yeast disappeared. With a catheter already in place, I didn't think that the treatment would be a problem. After the treatment started, I soon found that the drug made me nauseated. Several days passed before I was cured.

I was looking forward to my transfer to Valley Medical Center. My hopes were high for the first time since the accident. I had something to look forward to. I knew that was what I needed to get back on my feet.

A doctor from Valley Medical Center came to see me

and to talk to my Stanford doctor. He said that I wouldn't be transferred for days because a bed wasn't available there. He doubted that I could go through their rehabilitation program with my large bedsore. It would be difficult to go through their program without putting pressure on the sacral area, possibly enlarging and infecting the bedsore. I could feel my stomach sinking.

When John arrived, I told him the news. We had to wait to see if I would be accepted into the rehabilitation program and if a bed was available. Waiting was frustrating. The days passed slowly.

5

Valley
Medical Center

16

Valley Second Floor

Early on the morning of June 18th, after weeks of waiting, a doctor told me that I would leave that day for Valley Medical Center.

"It's about time," I thought. "I can't wait to leave. Once I start exercising, my body will begin to develop again."

I had taken great pride in keeping my body in good shape. I had done calisthenics and weightlifting at a health club several times a week. I had played tournament tennis and spent hours practicing. Most of all I loved dancing to music. When I had felt irritation, I would turn up the record player and dance it out of my body.

Now I was so anxious to start therapy, my frustration was at the boiling point. I knew that at first I wouldn't be able to work out or play tennis. Just sitting up would be a real challenge. I had to help myself.

John put my belongings in the car. A nurse, an ambulance driver, and his partner entered my room. They rolled a gurney next to my bed. My back was so sensitive that any movement was painful. I held my breath, hoping they knew what they were doing. It took three of them to transfer me from bed to gurney. The transfer wasn't as smooth as I had hoped. A nurse covered me with a blanket.

Some nurses came to say good-bye. There were a few tears. The driver pushed the gurney out of my room into the hall. I was on my way. We reached the emergency entrance and the doors opened for us. Then we were outside. It was a beautiful day. I couldn't remember when I had last been in the sun, over a month at least. The sun felt great, but the light was too bright. Closing my eyelids wasn't enough. I had to put my hands over my eyes.

As we reached the ambulance, John said, "I'll follow you to Valley Medical Center, Babe. See you there."

The ride to Valley was long. Every bump felt like a knife stabbing me in the back. When we finally arrived at the hospital and they lifted me out of the ambulance, I had to cover my eyes till we were inside. It was hard to believe that, when I had played tennis, I could serve into the sun.

We waited in the lobby of the Rehabilitation building a long time. The pain in my back was worse. The medication that I had received at Stanford was wearing off. I thought they would never take me to my room. I asked if anyone knew where we were going. The driver told me the second floor. After an elevator ride and several turns, we arrived at a nursing station.

"We've been waiting for you," said the head nurse. "Your room isn't ready yet, but we will put you in another room until yours is ready."

They wheeled me into an empty room, and, for a short time, I was alone. John had parked the car and finally found me. There was no phone in the room. I couldn't call my parents. John went to the Admissions Office to fill out the necessary billing forms.

After John returned, a nurse said that I would have some X-rays taken. Two nurses, with John's help, moved me onto a narrow, hard gurney. An orderly wheeled me to the elevator, with John following. We went down to the basement and along a narrow corridor. The orderly told someone in X-ray that I was there and then left me in the corridor with John. The gurney was hard. I was uncomfortable and in a lot of pain. I was covered only by a sheet and was cold. There was no railing to hold, so I couldn't pull myself on my side and off my bedsore. People were standing around me and constantly passing by. I was embarrassed to have no privacy.

After awhile, John asked someone when I would have my films taken. No one seemed to know. As time passed, John glared at radiology personnel that passed by. No one was concerned about me. After a forty-five minute wait, I was taken into a room with a large X-ray machine suspended from the ceiling. Painfully, I was moved onto the X-ray table. John put on a gown with lead shielding, so that he could stay in the room with me and hold me on my side, while they were taking X-rays of my knees and back. We waited while they developed the films. More films had to be taken and again we waited.

When we were told I could leave, we waited in the corridor for an orderly to come and take me to my room. I was in pain and very uncomfortable. John was irritated and decided not to wait. He wheeled me to the elevator and up to my room.

John found that the X-rays showed that my knees were fine, and the rods in my back were still in place. However, there was an increase in the angle between my sacrum and tailbone.

I was moved into a semi-private room with no wall decorations. Both beds were empty. In pain, I was placed in the bed next to the door.

John held my hand and said, "I'll get the nurse to give you something for the pain."

No orders had yet been written, and it took some time for the medication to arrive.

That afternoon the head of plastic surgery and two other doctors came by. They introduced themselves, examined my bedsore, and then re-bandaged me. I was told I wouldn't be admitted to the main floor for active rehabilitation, as long as I had a bedsore. The plastic surgeon planned to operate on me the next morning, moving some skin and muscle to cover the sore. After the surgery, I would remain on second floor for about six weeks, until the wound healed. He smiled and told me not to worry. He said he would see me in the morning.

John was surprised that the surgery had been scheduled so quickly. I was too tired to complain.

I sighed, closed my eyes, and whispered, "Dear God, I hope you know what you're doing."

Then I fell asleep.

That evening when my folks came, I told them the news. No one was happy that I was having more surgery. I was so upset, I couldn't eat or drink anything for dinner. My folks didn't stay long. They knew I was tired.

John held my hand and tried to comfort me. We talked awhile. I could tell John was as stressed as I was. I told him to go home and get some rest. He said he would return early in the morning.

17

Penny

Ten-thirty that night a psychologist named Penny visited me. She apologized for coming by so late. She often worked late and wondered if I would talk with her. I was delighted to have someone to talk to. I wasn't sleepy. She asked how I was doing and if I had emotional problems from the accident or the loss of my friends. We talked for some time.

"You know, Beverly, you're handling the accident quite well. I feel the main problem you have is your loss of independence. What I'm hearing is that you don't like depending on others."

"I'm an independent person. I'm basically a giver. I love doing things for others. To depend on family and friends is going to be hard to handle."

"What's it like when your friends come to visit?"

"Oh, I've asked my friends not to come by for a while. I couldn't let them see me like this, in so much pain. It's hard for my family to see me suffering. I know my friends are anxious to see me and want to help. I'm just not ready yet."

"Beverly, did you ever think that there are others who also get pleasure from giving? Actually, you would be giving by letting your friends visit you and do special things for you. Think about it. Wouldn't you feel good if you could help a friend in need? What a wonderful gift you would give them by letting them do something for you."

"I don't know, Penny, I'll have to think about it."

I enjoyed her company so much. She couldn't have come at a better time.

A little after eleven, my anesthesiologist came. He talked about the surgery and reminded me not to eat or drink **anything after midnight.**

"Oh, great. I haven't eaten all day."

I hadn't eaten much since the accident and seldom missed food. But being told I couldn't eat anything after midnight made me hungry.

Penny immediately asked, "Would you like me to run next door to Wendy's and get you a hamburger and a drink?"

"Are you kidding? At this hour of the night?"

"Wendy's is open all night long. I'll run over while you talk to the doctor. I'll be back in a jiffy."

The doctor sat next to my bed and told me about the anesthetic he would use on me. I stopped listening to what he was saying. Over and over in my mind I heard, "Don't let them put you to sleep."

I finally blurted out, "No, you can't use that on me. If you do the surgery, it has to be done under a local anesthetic."

I surprised him. He put down his clipboard and pencil.

"Why?" he asked.

"If you put me under, I won't wake up."

"What makes you think that?"

"My body is depleted of nutrients. I've lost thirty pounds or more. I have nothing left to fight with. I know I won't wake up if you put me to sleep."

I don't know why I said that. I hadn't thought about my condition before the conversation. It was as if someone was telling me to say those things. I was very calm. I knew what I had said was true. I don't know how I knew; I just did.

He hesitated a moment and then said, "I'll talk to the surgeon about it."

"Thank you. I'd appreciate it."

He left.

Penny arrived with burger and drink in hand. It was about 11:30, and I felt hungry for the first time in months. Maybe it was the wonderful smell of hamburger. I couldn't get the wrapper off fast enough. I hadn't had junk food in years. As I held the burger in my hands, I could feel the heat and see steam rising from the burger. It looked wonderful: the warm bun, juicy meat, lettuce, tomato, pickle, and all that sauce oozing down my hands. Lying on my side made eating a challenge, but I didn't care how messy I got. The first bite was like heaven. I closed my eyes and chewed. I couldn't believe I was eating and really enjoying it. My first real meal! I ate half the burger and drank most of the 7-up.

I turned to Penny, and said, "You're an angel. I don't know how I would have survived without you. I can't thank you enough."

She smiled and said, "The pleasure was all mine."

I looked at the twinkle in her eye and said, "Got it."

I understood what she meant. I had given her a chance to feel good about doing something for me. She said good night and left.

18

Awaiting Surgery

"I guess I'm going to be alone," I thought.

The overhead light was not very bright. The TV hanging from the ceiling was on, but there was static coming from it, and I couldn't hear the words. The noise irritated me, so I turned the TV off. The room was silent. I was uneasy. My pain was worse. I needed medication. I pressed the button for the nurse. It seemed forever before she appeared, and I took some medicine. I finally fell asleep, but not for long. At 1:15 in the morning a nurse came in to put an intravenous catheter in the back of my left hand, so it would be in place for my surgery that morning. It took several attempts before it was finally in. It hurt like hell, as fluid slowly dripped into my hand. I slept fitfully through the rest of the night. My hand hurt, and I wasn't looking forward to the operation.

In the morning, when John arrived, he saw that my hand was markedly swollen from fluid leaking around the needle. He went to get the nurse. She said that she couldn't adjust it or remove it without a doctor's approval. The resident was not on the floor, and the plastic surgeon was already in surgery. John went to find out when I would be taken to surgery. He found that I was a "to follow" case, so when I would go to surgery was indefinite. My hand hurt terribly. John was upset that nothing was being done about it.

Finally, at ten o'clock a nurse came to say that my surgery had been cancelled. She removed the IV from my hand. What a relief!

That afternoon the plastic surgeon and two residents came by.

"Well, Mrs. Differding, we have good news for you. We've decided not to operate. We'll watch the bedsore closely and hope that it will heal on its own."

I was so excited, I grabbed his hand and kissed it.

"Thank you, doctor. Does this mean I can start therapy?"

"I believe so. I'll get in touch with your rehab doctor and tell him that you're ready. Rehabilitation will be difficult for you, because you will have to do your exercises on your sides only. You must stay off your back."

I assured him that I could handle it. He smiled and gave my hand a squeeze.

"Thanks, doctor."

When he left, John turned to me and said, "I wonder why they cancelled your surgery."

I told John what I had said to the anesthesiologist the night before.

He shook his head and said, "You're unbelievable. I guess they listened to you. Someone must be watching over you."

"I know they are," I replied.

I was relieved not to have more surgery. I wanted to start therapy. I needed to participate in my healing. I wanted to improve my mobility and sit up. Two months of lying on my sides felt like two years. I wasn't sure what I could do. I was anxious to find out.

The next morning at nine, the doctors made rounds. Two young physicians entered my room.

"Good morning," said one. "I'll be working with you while you're on this floor."

He had a pleasant smile and very blue eyes.

"Did you have a good night's sleep?" asked the other doctor.

"I was a little restless and had a lot of pain."

"How is the pain this morning?"

"I still have it."

"It's rehab policy to give patients as little pain medication as possible. We'll start cutting down on yours today."

I didn't argue. I didn't want to do anything to jeopardize my chances of getting into rehab. I had waited long enough.

The doctor with the nice smile asked if I had any questions.

"When can I start?"

"Well, not for a while. We have a few things to check out first. Also, you have to be fitted for a back brace before we can transfer you to rehab. You can't sit up without it."

"How long will I have to wear the brace?"

"Five or six months, depending on how well you heal. Someone will come and fit you for the brace."

I was disappointed. I wanted to start therapy NOW! I had expected that once I was in this hospital, I would start rehabilitation. Here I was, still lying on my side.

19

Bleeding

Later that morning five plastic surgery doctors came to check my bedsore. They rolled me over and exposed my backside. Talk about letting it all hang out. That was bad enough. As they stood behind me, I heard: "Humm," "Unbelievable," "That's very large," "How long has it been like that," and "Look at this."

I hadn't been able to see my bedsore, which was fine with me. From all their comments, I imagined it was a pretty awful sight. One asked if I could feel them touching the sore.

"I can't feel anything."

"Good. We need to clean it up. We have to scrape away the dead tissue. Since you can't feel anything, we won't have to give you anything for the pain." They started to poke around. It didn't hurt, but I could feel pressure. The thought of them scraping my open sore made me sick.

Finally, someone said, "Okay, that should do it." They picked up four four-inch-square pieces of gauze, dipped them in some solution, and pressed them into the sore. They covered the gauze with a thick pad and taped it to me.

"We will have to do this every day till we get it under control. Be sure you don't lie on your back. It's important that you don't put pressure on the sore."

"So what's new?" I thought. "I haven't been allowed to lie on my back for over six weeks."

As they started to leave, I asked when I could start therapy.

"We're not sure. You still may need surgery."

"What kind of surgery?"

"If the bedsore doesn't get better, you may need a muscle and skin transplant. If we do that, it will take five to six weeks to heal. Don't get upset, Mrs. Differding. We haven't decided that surgery is the answer. We have to wait and see."

He smiled, said good-bye, and with the others left the room. I was shocked. I couldn't believe what I had heard. Another five to six weeks before I could get into rehab! More surgery! That would be six surgeries in eight weeks! I began to cry. When will this end?

A few hours later, I tried to roll over on my other side. As I did, my hand touched something wet. I strained to look behind me. The sheets were covered with blood. What had happened? I rang for the nurse. When she arrived and saw the blood, she told me that the bedsore was bleeding.

"I'll get the doctor right away."

The doctor arrived, removed the bandage, and examined the sore. He had to cauterize it to stop the bleeding. The smell was nauseating. When the doctor finished, he repacked the wound and left. The nurse cleaned me up and changed the sheets. Shortly after I was cleaned up, my folks came to visit. I felt sick and lightheaded. I was so weak I could barely speak.

As I looked at Mom, I whispered, "I don't feel well."

I could tell I was going to pass out. I could see my folks and hear their voices, but I couldn't talk. Their voices sounded further and further away. I felt as if I were spinning. That's all I remember.

92

When I awoke, a doctor, a nurse, and my folks were standing around the bed. When I asked what had happened, they told me I had fainted. I heard the nurse tell the doctor that my blood pressure was only 70/30. As the doctor looked through my chart, John arrived. The doctor told John that because of bleeding from my bedsore, my blood pressure had dropped, and I had fainted. The doctor ordered an intravenous catheter to be put in at once, so they could give me fluids.

Because everyone had been having a difficult time sticking my veins with a needle, I dreaded another attempt.

A nurse came into the room to put an IV in me. She asked John and my folks to wait in the hall. As she looked for a vein in one of my arms, I told her that I didn't have any good ones left.

"Don't worry," she replied. "I'm an expert at this."

She finally decided on a vein in the back of my hand. As she stuck the needle in, I gritted my teeth.

"Oh, dear, you moved, and I missed the vein. Now don't move this time."

She stuck me again and missed. The pain was unbearable. Again, she accused me of moving.

"I'm not moving," I cried.

"You certainly are. If you weren't, I wouldn't have missed."

I hadn't moved at all. When she put the needle in for the third time and missed again, I couldn't stand it any longer.

I screamed, "John, make her stop!"

John came into the room and said, "That's enough."

"Well, I don't appreciate someone yelling in my ear. She keeps moving and making me miss the vein."

I assured John that I hadn't moved. John told the nurse

to get out and send in a doctor. In a few minutes the doctor with the nice smile came in.

"I hear the nurse is having a little problem finding a vein. Well, don't worry. I'm a surgeon, and I've done this a lot."

He looked at my arms and then my hands. The hand that the nurse had worked on was badly swollen.

"Your other hand looks like it has a couple of good veins. I'm going to use a smaller needle. We shouldn't have any more problems." After his fourth unsuccessful try, with John watching, he looked up at me and said, "You're the first person I've not been successful with. We'll have to think of another way to give you nutrition."

When he left, I was totally exhausted. The tops of both hands were swollen and turning black and blue. John looked as exhausted as I felt. I began to cry.

"What's going to happen to me if I can't get any food down? I've already lost thirty pounds. I've never been this thin. The skin is hanging from my bones."

"Don't worry, Babe, you're still able to take fluids by mouth. Things will work out."

"I hope so," I whispered.

20

The Air Bed

Later that afternoon an air bed was brought in for me to keep as much pressure off my bedsore as possible. I don't like air beds. They're noisy and hot. This bed was exceptionally hot. I asked the nurse to lower the temperature of the bed. She fussed with it for awhile, and then said she couldn't do it. She would have someone from the bed company come and fix it.

I kept the covers off, but still found the bed uncomfortable. The plastic wraps squeezing my lower legs every few seconds were tight, hot, and made my legs sweat. I was supposed to keep them on most of the day and all night to help prevent blood clots in my legs. I was miserable enough without a hot bed and leg wraps. I learned how to reach the Velcro straps at the top of the boots. I would pull on them until the wraps came off. I did this when the nurses weren't around, which was most of the time. I hoped that someone would come to turn the heat down on the bed.

About eleven that evening, I noticed my lower abdomen was swelling. I was uncomfortable. I sensed something was wrong. I rang for the nurse. No one responded. I hated being alone in the evenings. It was so difficult to get a nurse. I kept ringing, and still no one came. I called John at home.

"John, my abdomen is swelling and it hurts. I can't get a nurse to come. What'll I do? I'm scared."

"Hang on, babe. I'll get dressed and get there as soon as I can."

He arrived in about twenty minutes. Still no nurse had come. John went to get someone. When a doctor examined me, it was obvious that my bladder was swelling. A catheter was put in my bladder and 950 cc. removed. (That's about twice the amount the bladder can safely hold. An over-distended bladder can rupture.) Someone had taken out my bladder catheter and not written orders for me to be catheterized regularly. Fortunately, I wasn't seriously damaged.

The following day a man from the air bed company came. He looked at the bed, and told the nurse that 82 degrees was as low as it could be set. No one knew what to do about it. There weren't any other air beds available in the hospital. I continued to sweat.

The next day my doctor came. He was concerned that I might develop blood clots in my legs. He knew that the air bed was too hot, and that I had been taking the intermittent pressure cuffs off my lower legs. "Because you can't move your legs, there is a danger of clots forming. Since the pressure cuffs are too hot for you to keep on, I'm going to prescribe heparin for you. The nurse will give you a shot every evening. I'm sorry. I know how you feel about needles, but this is important."

I sighed, and then told him I understood. A nurse came to give me the shot. I didn't realize that heparin was injected into the abdominal muscles. I was surprised how painful the injection was. I thought I didn't have any feeling there. The thought of being stuck in the abdomen was unnerving enough. Now I had to look forward to that every evening. What else could they do to me? I wondered if I would ever get to rehab.

I was still losing weight. I couldn't sit up, and I had trouble eating lying down. I really disliked the hospital food; the thought of it made me sick. The Wendy's burger was the only food I had enjoyed since the accident. I knew I needed to eat more, but it was hard to keep the hospital food down. I had to force myself to eat.

The doctor prescribed Ensure, a special drink high in nutrition. It was thick like a milkshake but not as good. I was to drink four cans of it a day. I managed to finish the first can. It wasn't great, but it was better than the hospital food, and a hell of a lot better than having a needle stuck in the back of my hand.

My family knew how much I disliked the hospital food. Either my folks would bring in food from a nearby fast food restaurant or my son and his wife would bring me food from home. I really looked forward to their visits and a chance to eat something I liked. I hated to have them leave at night. It was so lonely.

At eleven o'clock one night, a nurse came to give me my medication. She couldn't speak English well, but she smiled a lot. She told me she was supposed to clean my ostomy bag. I said fine.

"How do they do it?" she asked with a smile.

I talked her through the procedure and was happy when she left. I couldn't believe they had sent in a nurse who wasn't familiar with the procedure. I was pleased with myself for being patient with her.

The situation didn't get better. The night nurses on my floor had trouble speaking and understanding English. It made me uncomfortable. One came in to clean and bandage my bedsore. I rolled over to the side of the bed and held onto the railing, so I wouldn't slide back. I waited a few minutes for her to do something.

"How do they do this?" she asked.

I tried to stay calm. I told her I couldn't help her. Since I couldn't look behind me, I had never seen how it was done. I told her to get another nurse. A half hour later she returned smiling. She assured me that she now knew how to do it. I doubted it.

When she was through, I asked her to turn off the overhead light. She stood at the end of the bed looking at me quizzically. Then she smiled and nodded her head. She quickly pulled the covers over me and left the room, with the light still on. I couldn't believe it. Obviously, she had no idea what I had said.

Something as simple as moving covers to the end of the bed is very difficult when you can't sit up or move your legs. I was much too hot with them on. At that hour of the night it often took twenty minutes to an hour for a nurse to respond. I struggled to remove my blankets. By the time they were off, I was exhausted. I couldn't do anything about the overhead light, so I put a pillow over my head and tried to sleep.

The next day I noted that the skin beneath my ostomy bag was raw. Thinking about it made me so ill that I lost my lunch. A nurse came to bandage the sore, so the bag didn't rest on it. One more thing to add to the list. What else could go wrong?

An orthopedic surgeon came to examine me. He said that, before I could go to rehab, I would need a molded body brace with airholes and cutouts for my ostomy and my bedsore. He told me to avoid any twisting or flexion of my back. That was a laugh. The only way I could turn from side to side was by holding onto the side of the bed and pulling myself into position. I couldn't do that without twisting my back. Finally, a week after I entered the hospital, the bracefitter arrived. I didn't know how he would fit me, but I knew it wouldn't be easy. He gave the nurse instructions and then left the room. The nurse removed my nightgown. Over my head and around my body, she placed what looked like a giant tube sock with the toes cut out. She rolled me on one side and placed towels under me. The bracefitter returned with a bucket of water and several rolls of gauze. He immersed the plaster-coated gauze in the water, squeezed water out, and began wrapping me up like a mummy. Around and around he went from the armpits down to my hips. It wasn't too uncomfortable until the plaster started to harden. As it hardened around my chest, I felt I couldn't breathe. My breaths were shallow and fast, like a dog panting. I was worried. He assured me that, in a few more minutes, he would cut the cast off. That made me fearful that my skin would be cut. I had never had a cast removed, and I had no idea how he would do it. Suddenly, he turned on an instrument that looked like an electric saw. He explained how it worked. Was I glad when the cast was finally removed. I asked how long it would take to make my brace. He said he wasn't sure, maybe a week. That meant another week till I would be able to start rehab.

Later that day I got a pleasant surprise. I was finally transferred to a regular bed with an eggcrate mattress, so named because it has many indentations, like the containers that eggs come in, and was made of foam rubber. What a relief to be in a quiet, cool bed.

21

Awaiting Rehab

The following day my occupational therapist came to see me. She introduced herself, and said she would be working with me when I moved downstairs to rehab.

"Right now, I need some information, such as your weight and height, so I can fit you for a wheelchair."

She asked a few more questions and then left the room. She was a pretty young gal with much energy and enthusiasm. Compared to the way I felt, even a turtle would have seemed energetic.

At dinner time Mom and Dad showed up with a Wendy's burger, a bag of fries, and a 7-up. I ate everything. At last, I was enjoying eating again. I knew it was important to regain weight and strength for the rehabilitation ahead.

Pain in my legs and feet was a continual problem. I often had tingling and burning in both feet. Sometimes, I had shooting pains in my feet that drugs couldn't control. One day I complained to Penny. She offered to give me acupressure, which helped.

The next morning, while John was there, a nurse came to get me ready for breathing class. I was indignant. I knew I didn't have a breathing problem. I also didn't want to be wheeled downstairs in my bed in front of other people.

"I'm not going," I told the nurse.

She said the choice was up to me and left.

When one of the doctors heard that I refused to go, he told

John how important it was that I participate in all the classes.

John tried to persuade me to change my mind. "Come on, babe, give it a try. I'll go with you to class."

I reluctantly agreed to go. John offered to help take me downstairs and off we went. It was embarrassing to be wheeled down the halls in a bed. When we arrived, I felt a little better to see other patients had also come in their beds. There were about twelve patients in wheelchairs and five of us in beds. They wheeled me next to a young man who was in bad shape. He was strapped in a rotator bed that could be rolled from side to side. He had casts on one arm and one leg. He wore a halo, a metal ring around the head that supports the neck and is held in place by screws that are embedded in the skull. He smiled, introduced himself, and asked my name. He seemed fairly happy, which amazed me. He asked what had happened to me, and I told him.

He told me that he had been hiking up a cliff and fell, breaking his neck, arm, and leg. "I have no one to blame but myself. It was all my fault. I'm lucky to be alive."

As his bed was rolled to the other side, I whispered to John, "I think he has brain damage. Did you notice how happy he was? He's in terrible shape and doesn't know it. I think he's gone loony tunes."

The room filled up. Several therapists were there.

"Everyone settle down," said one therapist. "We have a new patient with us today. Her name is Bev. Please say 'Hi' to Bev."

Everyone harmonized, "Hi, Bev."

I wanted to slide under my blanket, but I smiled. Next, the therapist had them tell me their names.

I was thinking, "I really don't need this."

I was amazed that almost everyone seemed in good spirits. I wasn't.

For the first exercise, everyone took a deep breath and then counted as high as he could before taking another breath. I was the last to finish, counting into the forties. Everyone had stopped long ago, and all were staring at me. I was embarrassed and felt that maybe they thought I was cheating. I did all the exercises without any problem. When the class was over, orderlies or nurses came to take the patients back to their rooms. I was left alone with John, waiting to be taken back to my room.

"I told you I didn't need this class."

"In Palm Springs you had a difficult time breathing because of the pain. No one since then has really checked your breathing capacity or given you breathing exercises to prevent pneumonia. The therapists here have to see how well you can do."

"I don't have any problem breathing. I did well in class. Surely, they noticed. Maybe, now they'll move me to a class where I can work on walking."

"One thing at a time, Babe. Remember, you can't even sit up yet. There are a lot of stages that you will have to go through before you will be ready to attempt walking."

I didn't say anything. I knew he was right. I had a lot of hard work ahead of me. Finally, with John at my side, I was wheeled back to my room. We talked awhile, and then he left.

My doctor stopped by to tell me there was a good possibility that I would be moving to rehab in a few days. I was afraid to get too excited, for fear I'd be disappointed again. I had expected to go to rehab when I left Stanford nine days ago.

"Bev, I know you've had a rough time of it. You really ought to take advantage of the time you have here. Once you're in rehab, they're going to work your butt off. To stay there, you must put in three hours of therapy a day. The only time you're allowed to miss a class is if you're on your death bed. You won't be treated like patients in the rest of the hospital. They don't consider you ill. You're there to work. It isn't quiet either. Sometimes, radios will be playing loudly. There are four patients to a room, and there's a lot of kidding around and laughing. No one is going to feel sorry for you. They expect you to do for yourself. This is part of the therapy. You need more people around you. It will be good for you. Also, ask John to bring you some clothes from home. You're not allowed to stay in your gown during the day. Sweats and tennis shoes are best."

I listened carefully. He had been so kind to me. I would miss him when I left. We talked awhile longer, and then he left. When I saw John, I told him what the doctor had said. In the middle of our conversation, the occupational therapist arrived with a wheelchair.

"Good morning," she said with a smile. "Look what I've got for you."

I couldn't believe how enthusiastic this person was over a wheelchair.

"Well, what do you think?" Before I could say anything, she continued, "Isn't it great? It's your very own wheelchair. I thought the red color was pretty snazzy. You can race around the halls in style."

If she only knew what I was thinking! Riding around town in my red Honda Prelude was snazzy, not cruising the halls of the hospital in a stupid red wheelchair. I wanted to tell her to take her chair and shove it, right out the window.

I tried not to get angry. It wasn't her fault I needed a wheelchair. She was just young and enthusiastic, trying hard to do her job.

John joined in, "Gee, Hon, isn't this nice. I'll bet you'll be happy to get out of bed and into this chair."

I wanted to tell him that he lost the bet. I no more wanted to get in that damn chair, than I wanted to be in this stupid bed. I wanted to walk! I held my tongue. A dirty look at John and the silent treatment for the therapist were better than anything I could have said. She turned and pushed the chair toward the door.

"Your chair will be kept outside by your door. Your name is taped on it so no one will take it by mistake. See you in rehab."

As she left, I felt that I had burst her bubble.

"What's the matter, Babe, don't you like your chair?"

"Why is everybody so excited about getting me in that stupid wheelchair? I hope you know that it's only temporary. Once I build up my muscles, I'll be able to walk again. Everybody around here thinks I'm going to be glued to a wheelchair for life!"

"Now, Babe, don't get excited. We're only trying to help. Being in a wheelchair isn't that bad. There's a lot of things you can do from a chair."

"There you go again, talking negatively. I don't want to hear about what I can do in that thing. You don't believe I'm going to be able to walk, but I will. I don't want to hear another word about that wheelchair."

I knew John was trying to be helpful, but that was something I didn't want to hear. We didn't talk about it again. With me John had the patience of a saint.

Later that day, a nurse told me I would go to rehab the

next day. She had several paper bags with her.

"I'll pack most of your belongings now."

She filled the bags and lined them up by the wall.

"It's really happening," I thought. "Now I can get excited."

When morning came, I waited for the nurses to come and move me downstairs. At 9 AM my breakfast tray was brought in.

"Maybe after breakfast they'll move me," I thought.

A nurse came in and began to unpack my bags. "What's happening?"

"I'm sorry, but rehab can't take you yet. They're short of nurses. If you went down now, no one would be available to take care of you."

Another disappointment! This was ridiculous. I was so frustrated I began to cry.

"Oh, don't cry, Mrs. Differding. They think they'll have a full staff by tomorrow."

Two more days passed, and nothing happened. The doctor came to tell me he was filling out my transfer papers for the third time. He was sure I would be leaving that day. A nurse came to pack my belongings again. I waited and waited. Just before lunch, the doctor returned.

"Bev, I hate to tell you this, but there's not a bed available for you. The patient that was to leave today has to stay for another day or two."

That was the last straw. I called John at work. I could barely speak. Tears were streaming down my face as I told him what had happened. He tried to reassure me.

Shortly afterward, my friends Betty and Judy walked in, lunch in hand, to find me hysterical. Betty came over, held my hand, and asked what was wrong. I tried to tell them, but they had trouble understanding me through the sobs.

I kept repeating, "They keep saying I can move to rehab, and then they say I can't. I'm never going to get better if they don't let me start therapy."

Betty excused herself and stormed to the nurse's station. She demanded to see my doctor. The nurse told her he was with another patient, but would come to my room when he was through. Betty returned to my room, followed by the head nurse.

"What seems to be the problem?" she asked.

"Bev needs help and needs it fast. She's hysterical. She doesn't know why she's not being allowed to start therapy. Someone better give her some answers."

"The doctor should be here soon," replied the nurse as she turned and left the room.

A few minutes later, the bracefitter walked in. He was immediately assailed by my friends who thought he was the doctor. He explained who he was, and that he had just come to tell me that my brace would be ready in a few days. He told them that it wouldn't do me any good to be in rehab until he finished my brace, because I wouldn't be allowed to sit up without it.

I began to calm down. I felt badly that my friends had seen me this way. I didn't like people to see me cry. Judy got up and said she would be back in a few minutes. Apparently she went to encourage the nurse to hurry the doctor. When she returned, we ate lunch. I had worked up an appetite with all my sobbing. I ate everything.

When the doctor finally appeared, my friends told him what they thought of my situation. He explained that I hadn't been ready for the move till now, and now there wasn't an available bed.

"Why didn't you explain that to her? She wouldn't have been so upset."

After my buddies left, the doctor returned and asked who they were. I explained that they were friends, who were upset to see me out of control.

"Well, I'm sorry I didn't explain things better. You'll be transferring in a day or two." I didn't say a word. Sometimes, silence says it all. "Your rehab physician will be coming by to talk with you. He's a real sweetheart; you'll like him a lot."

That evening my rehab physician did show up. He told me to pack. I was moving that night. Soon, everything was packed, and I was ready to go. Nurses came in and placed my belongings on top of my bed. They swung the bed around and pushed me towards the elevator. Whatever my friends had said had worked. I was on my way to rehab! Little did I know how great a challenge I faced.

6

Rehabilitation

22

Rehab at Last

It was about five PM on July 1st when two nurses took me down to my new room on the first floor, number 173. The room held four patients, and they parked my bed in slot D. The nurses said good-bye and left.

I looked around. My bed was close to the door and next to a wash basin with a large mirror over it. Directly across the room from the basin was the door to a large room containing a sink and toilet. The young woman in the bed directly across from me saw me looking at her.

"Hi, I'm Sandy, and that's Flo," pointing to the women next to her.

"Hi, I'm Bev. I came down from the second floor."

"We heard we were going to have company," said Sandy.

The bed next to me was empty.

"Is anyone in that bed?" I asked.

"No, not yet, but there will be soon. These beds are never empty for more than a day."

The whole scene seemed strange. It was like summer camp, and I was the new kid in the group. Flo didn't say anything; she just stared at me. Sandy and Flo were each wearing a halo, a steel ring that is placed around the head at the level of the forehead, about an inch away from the head. It's attached to the head by four screws that are actually drilled into the skull. The halo is supported by four steel rods that extend downward to a plastic ring that rests on the

111

shoulders. Patients with broken necks wear them so their head is supported and the head and neck don't move. They are worn until the neck has healed enough to be able to support the head.

I noticed that they had little or no use of their arms and hands and couldn't move their bodies without the help of a nurse. They were called quads (or quadriplegics), because all four extremities were paralyzed. Nevertheless, both were sitting up in bed. That was something I hadn't been able to do for over two months. Although I had more muscle function than they did, I didn't feel there was much difference between us.

On the wall behind and above each of their beds was a bulletin board filled with pictures, cards, and trinkets. Sandy's had a large poster of a woman in a bikini, flexing her muscles. I asked Sandy who the woman was.

"That's me. I had just won the 1986 Women's Champion Body Building contest."

It was hard to believe that she had once looked like that. Muscle atrophies rapidly when you can't move. I thought about how I must look. I hadn't been able to see myself in a mirror. Sandy was cute, about twenty-three years old, five feet tall, and now about eighty pounds. We exchanged stories of our injuries.

Sandy had fallen off a lifeguard stand into the shallow end of a pool, hitting her head on the bottom. She had broken her neck and, with no control of her body, had floated to the top of the pool face down. Fortunately, a friend had pulled her from the pool. The doctors had told her she would never be able to move from the neck down.

"They're full of it," she said. "I'm going to show them. In fact, I just wiggled my big toe this morning."

112

I knew right away I was going to like this feisty little gal. Flo hadn't said much. I asked what had happened to her.

"I was in a car accident. It was my fault. I was drunk and drove off the road. I broke my neck. My friend who was in the car was killed."

I had mixed feelings. I was sorry that she was hurt, but angry that she had been driving drunk. I wanted to say something about drunk drivers, but I didn't.

"That was my third car accident. All three times I was drunk. You'd think I would have learned."

I'm glad I hadn't said anything to her; it wouldn't have done any good.

She was bitter and angry. She was forty-five years old, but looked sixty. Her story was better than any novel I'd read. She told us she had been a porno model and a prostitute. She drank heavily and had started taking drugs at a young age. She had been at Valley for almost a year and hadn't improved.

At supper time, nurses transferred Sandy and Flo into their chairs, so they could wheel into the dining area and eat. Sandy had an ordinary wheelchair. It took her a long time to go anywhere, because she insisted on trying to move the chair with the little arm movement she had.

She would say, "If you don't use it, you lose it."

Flo had an electric chair and seemed content to do as little as possible.

I was jealous because I couldn't sit in a chair or even sit up in bed. I watched patients outside my door, wheeling back and forth, laughing and kidding with the nurses. I couldn't understand how anyone could have a good time in a place like this. Being paralyzed wasn't funny to me.

I eventually realized that laughing was a way to deal

with the situation. I joined in, by kidding around and occasionally having a good laugh. It would have been easy to focus on our loss of body function and feel sorry for ourselves. The nurses didn't treat us like sick patients, because we weren't. We were handicapped and were expected to do as much for ourselves as we could.

A nurse entered the room carrying my dinner tray. She set it on my table, told me to enjoy, and left. I leaned toward the table and lifted the cover off the plate. It was unappetizing. As I was about to take a bite, Mom and Dad arrived with Kentucky fried chicken and other goodies. They saved the night. Before the evening was over, my whole family (my folks, John, Gary, Stephanie and Ken) arrived to check out my new surroundings. I told everyone about my new roommates. Things looked better with my tummy full of chicken and my bed surrounded by loved ones. Sandy's parents came to visit, and everybody introduced themselves. It was like a celebration. I was finally in rehabilitation. Everyone stayed fairly late, and my family left with their spirits high. They had been as anxious for this move as I was. It had been a big day for me, and I was very tired. What I needed was a good night sleep.

Sleep didn't come easily. There was noise throughout the night. Nurses often talked and laughed just across the hall, and a door slammed repeatedly.

Seven-thirty the next morning, I was awakened by the nurses changing shifts. The two nurses for our room came in smiling and said good morning to us. I was tired and not ready for the cheerfulness. When I complained about the door slamming, Sandy explained that the supply room door automatically slammed shut when anyone went in or out. She told me I would get used to it. That was hard to believe.

A nurse brought me towels, a washcloth, a little bowl of warm water, and soap. She asked if I could bathe myself. I told her I could probably do the top half but not the bottom half. She told me to start, and she would come back to finish up. I was glad I could do some things for myself. My roommates had to depend on the nurses for almost everything. After my sponge bath, my breakfast arrived. It wasn't appetizing, but I needed to eat to keep up my strength. We all ate breakfast in bed. Sandy was supposed to wear hand braces to help her hold a fork to feed herself. She refused and managed quite well on her own. Flo had to have the nurse feed her.

After breakfast, the nurses dressed Sandy and Flo and sent them to their therapy classes. Without a back brace, I couldn't attend classes. I was by myself, lonely and frustrated. I wasn't any better off than I was when I was upstairs.

When the nurse came back to the room and saw my eyes full of tears, she said, "It's quiet in here with everyone at therapy. I know it's late in the morning, but would you like to have a shower?"

"Oh, I'd love one. I haven't had a shower since the accident. It's been nine weeks."

I didn't know how I could have a shower, but I was ready to try. I would have done anything to get out of bed.

"I know you will feel a lot better. I'll round up two more nurses to help lift you onto the gurney."

She returned with two nurses and a gurney covered with plastic, so water wouldn't damage it. The nurses lined up on one side of my bed. One slid her hands under my shoulders, another under my back, and the third under my knees.

"On the count of three," said my nurse. "One, two, three."

They lifted me, took several steps to the gurney, and placed me carefully on it. My nurse put a towel over me, and we were off to the showers. She wheeled me into the shower room and closed the door behind us. There were two stalls, and she wheeled me into one. She put oversized rubber boots over her shoes. I was anxious to feel warm water on my body and to shampoo my hair. She came into the shower stall, turned on the faucets, and waited for the water to warm up. She took the showerhead off the hook and began to spray me. The water quickly changed from warm to cold. I started to shiver, and my teeth chattered.

"Oh, Beverly, I'm so sorry. They must have used up all the hot water."

"That's okay," I stuttered. "A cold shower is better than no shower. Anyway, blue is a good color for me."

She dried me and wrapped me in several towels. Once I warmed up, I felt better. I thanked her, but she kept apologizing.

At lunchtime, everyone else went to the dining room to eat. I was again alone in the room. I couldn't wait till I would be able to eat a meal sitting up.

23

Therapy Begins

After lunch, someone came to see me.

"Hi, my name is Jill, and I'm going to be your physical therapist. Until you can sit in your chair, we'll do what we can in your bed. I'll start with some range of motion exercises."

"That sounds great to me. I'm anxious to get started."

"Once you can wheel yourself around, you'll have other therapists working with you throughout the day. You're expected to participate in at least three hours of therapy a day. If you don't, you'll be asked to leave. We have a lot of patients waiting to fill your bed."

I looked at her and thought, "I know. I was one of those waiting. You don't have to worry about me missing classes."

I felt better as she stretched my legs. At last, something was being done for my poor legs. When she finished, she told me that the nurses would be putting me in my chair every few hours, so I would build up my tolerance for sitting. I couldn't believe that sitting up could be such a problem. She told me that my class schedule would be posted on the bulletin board in the hall. I was to check it each day.

"Great," I thought. "My first challenge will be to sit up long enough to wheel out in the hall, so I can read the bulletin board."

Soon after Jill left, the man that had made my brace arrived.

"Well here it is," he said. "How do you like it?"

It looked gross. Heavy plastic with little holes all over.

"I don't care what it looks like, I just want to be able to sit up in it."

"You will be," he replied. "You can go to work now."

"Yeah," I thought. "It's about time."

About an hour later, the nurse told me it was sitting time. First, I had to put on my back brace. I rolled over to one side so she could put the back part of the brace under my back. Then I rolled back, so she could place the front part of the brace on my chest and pull the brace straps tight. I complained that it was too tight, but she didn't seem concerned. I couldn't take a deep breath, and yawning or sneezing were definitely out. I thought that having the brace on was all I needed to sit in my wheelchair. Was I wrong. The nurse said I needed to put on support-hose.

"Why in the world do I need to wear support-hose?" I asked.

"It helps keep your blood pressure from dropping so low that you faint."

After some effort, the nurse put them on. They looked like white elastic tube socks that reached my knees.

"Terrific," I thought. "Not only am I uncomfortable, but I look like something from another planet."

"We're ready. I'll get another nurse to help me move you into the chair."

They tilted the head of my bed up, and, for the first time in nine weeks, I was actually sitting. One nurse placed herself behind me, and put her arms under mine and around my chest. The other nurse lifted my legs, and, before

I knew it, I was in my wheelchair.

"All right," I thought. "I'm in my chair. I did it. What's so hard about sitting up?"

In a few minutes I began to sweat. I could feel the blood draining from my face. My support-hose was letting me down. The room spun, and I felt I would slide out of my chair onto the floor. Sitting was a lot harder than I thought it would be. I must have looked as bad as I felt. The last thing I remember was the shocked look on the nurse's face as she came rushing to my side. After I tried to sit several times and fainted each time, the doctor prescribed amphetamine to keep my blood pressure up. It worked. When I was finally able to sit up for thirty minutes, I was proud of myself.

As I wheeled around, I noticed everything was out of focus. Something was wrong with my eyes. When I told the doctor, he said my eyes needed time to adjust to looking at things from an upright position, and they would be fine in several days. It never occurred to me that lying flat for a long time would affect my vision. After a few days of practicing sitting in my chair, I would be able to attend all my classes. My tolerance for sitting was still not 100%, but it was good enough.

I still had leg and foot pain. I remembered the doctor upstairs said they didn't give pain medication in rehab. I hoped it would settle down and not interfere with my therapy.

When I attended breathing class in my chair for the first time, we were introduced to a new patient, Cathy. She had a neck injury, a head injury, and had lost a thumb in an automobile accident. With all her problems, she still smiled. I liked that and wanted to know her better.

After class, we talked in the hall. Cathy was a music

teacher. I immediately liked her. I told her of the empty bed next to mine, and that I hoped she would be transferred there. She said that she didn't like the room she was in and thought it would be nice to move.

Of the 40 patients on our ward, only five were women. That evening Cathy was assigned to our room. Her whole family flocked around her bed. She introduced them: husband, daughters, and mother-in-law. They were a lovely family. At night our room was filled with family and friends. No one ever came to visit Flo, so we all shared our family with her, along with the food everyone brought.

It was fun to have such lovely people fill our room.

Now that I was able to sit up and wheel around in my chair, Jill told me I was ready to go to physical therapy class. But first, I was to meet her in the gym to have my muscle function evaluated. When I wheeled to the gym, I found her waiting, with clipboard and pencil in hand.

"Okay, Bev, let's see how much function you have in those legs."

My legs had always been my strongest part. With so much pain, I was sure some of my muscles would work. She helped me transfer on to the mats. At least I no longer needed two nurses to lift me. I could now lean on one person and be transferred. I scooted back to the middle of the mat and sat there with my legs stretched out in front of me. Jill pushed my pant legs up. For the first time in months, I saw what was left of my beautiful muscular legs. It was hard to believe those pale, skinny legs belonged to me. I was shocked. As I ran my hand over them, my legs felt nothing. It was as if I were touching someone else. How could I feel so much pain in my legs and yet not feel my touch? As I stared at my legs, my eyes filled with tears.

"All right, let's go to work," said the therapist. "I want you to slide your right leg out to the side."

I looked down at my right leg and tried to move it, but nothing happened. No matter how hard I tried, it didn't move, not even a twitch. It was as if someone had strapped a hundred pound weight to each leg. I couldn't believe it. I tried harder and harder, till I was grunting and red in the face.

Jill put her hand on my shoulder and said, "Hey, Bev, slow down. Don't try so hard. There's no trophy involved here. It's just a muscle test."

She didn't know who she was talking to. I never did anything half-heartedly. I took pride in everything I did and worked as hard as I could. Right now, I was more frustrated than anything else. I couldn't believe that with so much mental effort, I still couldn't move anything. I hadn't thought I was that bad. It felt strange having half a body that didn't work. The top half was still me, but the bottom half belonged to someone else. It was sad to think of how muscular and athletic my legs had been. Dancing, weight lifting, and tennis had made my legs look great. I wondered how long it would take to get them back in shape.

After the testing I was extremely tired. I couldn't imagine using so much energy without accomplishing anything. I could barely move anything from the waist down, no matter how hard I tried. I was disappointed and frustrated. I wanted to scream as loud as I could. Instead, I held it in. I knew if I tried to say anything, I would burst into tears. The stress made my pain worse, and I wanted to lie down.

Jill said she would work out a program for me and post it on the bulletin board the next day. I would start each morning with my occupational therapist, Donna.

"Where do I meet Donna for therapy?" I asked.

121

"She'll come to your room and work with you there."

I headed for my room. I needed to sleep.

The next morning at nine, Donna, with all her enthusiasm, came to see me.

"Hi, Bev, how are you doing?"

"I'm hanging in."

"Good. I thought we could start today with getting dressed. How much can you do on your own?"

"I can do the top part, but not the bottom half. I can't reach my feet when I'm lying down."

"I think we might be able to solve that problem."

She showed me what looked like a 3-foot wooden handle with a hook on the end. She handed it to me and told me to put my sweat pants on the end of the hook and place them by my feet. I was able to do that. Then, using the hook, she wanted me to pull the pants over my feet and up my legs, till I could reach them with my hands. It sounded easy. On the first try, my toe got caught in the crotch of the pants. On the second try, I managed to get both legs into one pant leg. Each time, Donna had to help me. After many unsuccessful tries, Donna gave me a start by placing each foot in the proper pants hole. With the hook I was able to pull the pants up to where I could reach them with my hands. The next step was to pull them over my fanny. This wasn't easy. I couldn't lift my bottom at all. Donna told me that I could roll to one side and pull up and then roll to the other side and pull up. It took about six rolls from side to side before my pants were in the right place. Donna could tell I was frustrated.

"Don't worry, it gets easier after a while."

"I hope so. I'd hate to spend most of my time getting dressed and undressed."

"Let's see how you do with your shoes and socks."

"Do we have that much time left?" I asked.

"We'll give it a try. Can you bring your foot up at all?"

When she saw I couldn't, she tried to move it for me. She found that I didn't have enough bend in my knees.

"We'll start working on that tomorrow," she said.

She put my shoes and socks on and helped me transfer to my chair.

"By the way, tomorrow morning I'll bring you a sliding board to help you transfer on your own."

24

The Schedule

After Donna left, I wheeled to the bulletin board to see my schedule. The board was huge and nicely organized with everyone's name and schedule on it. I found my name and checked out my classes.

At 9:00 I had occupational therapy, which I had just finished.

The 10:00 breathing class I had attended each morning wasn't on my schedule. It had been replaced by "range of motion therapy." My 11:00 class was "wood shop." Wood shop didn't sound like anything I needed. That was probably a mistake.

Everyone had a two hour lunch.

At 2:00 I had "weightlifting" and at 2:30, "tilttable." From 3:00–4:00 I had "physical therapy." That was what I've been waiting for. At 4:00 everybody met in the day room for special training programs, such as bladder and bowel care and how to survive in the world of the handicapped.

They were going to keep me busy. I felt tired looking at all the things I had to do.

It was close to 10:00. I had to wheel to the gym for my range of motion therapy.

I thought range-of-motion would be good. I had liked it when Jill had worked my legs when I was unable to get out of bed.

I met Jill in the gym and she helped me transfer to the

mats. She introduced me to a 'range-of-motion strap,' a three foot strap with a loop at the bottom. I was to slip my foot into the loop, hold the other end, and lean back on the mat. Then I was to pull my leg straight up in the air. It wasn't easy. My leg was heavy and I had no control of it. When I tried to pull my leg up, it weaved from side to side. Jill wasn't watching me. My leg fell to one side with a large thud and I screamed with pain.

I was angry with Jill and told her she should help me. She insisted I could do it by myself. She said I needed to concentrate. She showed me a few more strap exercises. I was incapable of doing the exercises properly without her help, and she wouldn't help me. That made me angry. I knew I had to work with her daily, so I tried to be nice and apologized for getting angry. I knew how dependent and vulnerable I was. I couldn't afford to have her dislike me.

My next class was wood shop. Jill told me how to get there. I had to take the elevator down. I wheeled to the elevator, pushed the button, and waited alone for it to arrive. I had hoped someone would be with me for my first ride in an elevator. When the doors opened, no one was in the elevator. I took a deep breath and wheeled in. When the doors closed, I was nervous and started to sweat. I wondered what I would do if the elevator didn't work. Fortunately, I only had to go down one floor so the ride was quick. Was I relieved when the doors opened!

I wheeled to the room number I had been given. As I entered, the teacher asked if I was Beverly, and I said yes. He pointed to an empty space at a long table. There were about seven of us in the class, all spinal cord patients. I was given a folder to look through and find something I might like to construct. I didn't understand why I needed this class. It wouldn't help my legs.

I picked a small planter box that looked fairly easy to make. One of my classmates, Chuck, was a whiz at carpentry. He was making a large bird house, which looked professionally done. I knew I couldn't do as well as he, and as you might have guessed, I had to sit next to him. Heaven only knew what my little planter box would look like next to his fabulous bird house.

We did much sawing, sanding, hammering, and staining. I wasn't very proficient, but it did help build up my upper body. I developed arm muscles I never knew existed. The teacher was easygoing and we all kidded each other. It was a pleasant time that we all needed. Our other classes were stressful.

When wood shop was over, the teacher walked with us to the elevator. At times he rode the elevator with us. I liked that.

After wood shop I was tired. I was glad when it was lunch time so that I could rest for two hours before my next class.

At 2:00 I had weightlifting class in the gym. The physical therapist (PT) was an enthusiastic muscular fellow named Dave. He had the six of us form a circle with our wheelchairs. He gave each of us one-pound weights and gave us exercises that would strengthen our arms. We moaned and groaned with each new exercise he had us do. He explained we needed those muscles to push our chairs. He said if we didn't stop complaining, he would tell us some of his jokes. After the first few jokes, we booed and hissed and promised we wouldn't complain anymore. Dave made our class fun and challenging. Once a week we had wheelchair races in the hospital corridors. Dave would stand at the end of the hall with his stop watch and wave us on at the other end, one at a time. I enjoyed competing and beat several of the guys. My classmate Chuck was very upset when he lost to me.

Dave told him, "Don't feel bad, Chuck. After all, it's easier for Bev. She weighs less and therefore she can wheel faster."

I don't think Chuck bought that. I later found him in the gym, pumping iron on his own time. I enjoyed seeing him trying to improve. I wished more patients had his determination. Some patients didn't care or try to get better. Sometimes PT's had to go to patients' rooms and take them to the gym. Other patients just went through the motions, not putting any effort in what they were doing.

I didn't understand why they weren't trying. I was. I wouldn't miss a class if I could help it.

The next half hour in the gym was spent on the tilttable, a long table with several straps around it and a footrest at one end. Jill and Dave helped me transfer onto the table and had me lie down with my feet against the footrest. After I was strapped to the table, Jill turned a knob that slowly tilted the table. Fortunately, they only tilted me a little the first time. I began to sweat and I could feel the blood drain from my head. I saw spots in front of my eyes and became very dizzy. When I thought I would lose my lunch, someone came over and lowered the head of the table. By the end of the week I was able to tolerate being in a vertical position. It sounds easy, but after being horizontal for three months, it's quite challenging. Weeks passed before I felt normal in an upright position. The tilttable made my pain worse.

When a patient was on the tilttable for the first time, his face would change from white to pale gray. When he turned green, the PT returned him to a horizontal position.

When I was taken off the tilttable I wheeled over to the mats for my most important class, physical therapy, with a pleasant therapist, Heather. For thirty minutes she helped me bend, lift, slide, and push my legs around, movement I was unable to do on my own. My greatest frustration was the constant pain which kept me from doing my best. In spite of it, I tried hard.

Then another PT, Sarah, worked on my balance in a sitting position. She helped me scoot to the end of the mat and placed my legs over the side. Sitting on the edge of the mat wasn't too difficult, as long as I kept my hands on the mat to keep me from swaying. She picked up a large beach ball. She told me she was going to throw the ball to me and I was to catch it. Before I could say anything, she threw the ball. To my surprise, I caught the ball. I started to wobble. I dropped the ball and placed my hands on the mat so I wouldn't fall. She congratulated me for the nice catch. Next I was to catch the ball and throw it back to her.

Even when I was successful, I was constantly afraid I would fall. With no feeling in my fanny, I couldn't tell if I was leaning forward or back or to one side or the other. That was the longest thirty minutes of the day.

After a few weeks my classes were pretty routine. I'd received many cards and letters since the accident. They meant so much to me, to know that people cared. Friends called to see if I was ready for visitors. Most asked if I needed anything and wanted to help me if they could. I remembered what Penny had said about letting my friends do things for me. So, even though I was often in pain, I encouraged visiting.

I had free time during the lunch hour. Since I didn't like hospital food, I asked visitors if they would mind bringing lunch. We could talk as we ate. As soon as the word spread, I had visitors and excellent lunches Monday through Friday.

Penny was right. My friends were happy doing things for me, and I certainly enjoyed their company and great lunches. Visiting with my friends in the middle of the day was a pleasant way of breaking up the hard work days.

I enjoyed the evenings that were spent with my family. I became comfortable at the hospital. Some of the patients and nurses were my good friends. I believe most of the patients felt that way.

25

The X-Rated Movie

Monday through Thursday at 4:05 all of us recent paraplegic and quadriplegic patients met in the ward's dayroom for lectures on spinal cord injury care.

Evelyn, the nurse in charge, talked about bowel and bladder function and care: what changes had resulted from our accidents and how we could deal with these on a day-to-day basis when we left the hospital. We were told how to look for signs of urinary tract infection, which is the most common cause of hospitalization and death in paraplegics and quadriplegics. Sometimes we had visitors come to talk to us, people who had suffered spinal cord injuries, like us, and were back living productive lives.

But some of the things Evelyn showed us were inappropriate. We viewed slides and movies of activities that could be done from a wheelchair, such as riding a chair down a mountain, or even downhill skiing. Much of the lectures were about advanced athletic activities that most of us didn't want to think about and could never accomplish.

We were still trying to get over the shock of our accidents, and adjust from being healthy, active, and often athletic adults to being disabled. Most of the people in the ward, unlike me, were quadriplegic, and it was difficult for them just to move their chairs.

One day Evelyn told us that we would have three

lectures on how spinal cord patients could have sex, and then at the end of the week, a movie on the subject. She sounded excited about the movie, but wouldn't tell us anything about it other than it was X-rated. Sandy and I looked at each other and chuckled. We thought she was kidding. I had never seen an X-rated movie or even had the desire to see one. Evelyn told us that anyone missing one of the lectures wouldn't be allowed to see the movie.

The day for the movie came, and patients in wheel-chairs filled the dayroom. Everyone was talking and laughing. The three women, Sandy, Cathy, and I, sat together, with about 36 male patients and guests packed into the room around us. Flo had decided not to go to the movie. She was only interested in getting pain medication from the doctors, but because she had been an addict prior to her accident, she wasn't allowed narcotics and spent most of her time complaining.

Evelyn had told us that we could invite our husbands, wives, girlfriends or boyfriends to the movie. None of the women had invited guests, but many of the men had, so the room was crowded. Everyone appeared anxious for the movie to begin. But once it started, there was shocked silence in the room.

First, a young couple appeared on the screen with a voice introducing them as a young male quadriplegic and his girlfriend who had no disabilities. The girlfriend undressed, wheeled the man close to the side of the bed, and pushed him out of his chair onto the bed, where she began to undress him. Sandy, who was sitting next to me, pushed my arm, and when I turned to look at her, her eyebrows were raised almost to her hairline. We made funny faces at each other, like teenagers, because we were uncomfortable, not because what was taking place on the screen was a laughing matter. We were embarrassed and uneasy. What was being shown was humiliating and degrading. Although we needed to learn how our injuries would affect our sex lives, this was the wrong way to do it.

On the screen now, both the man and the woman were undressed. The man still had a catheter attached to his penis. I didn't watch at this point, but wondered how they could have sex. The next time I looked up, the man was having spasms, his entire body jerking rapidly and uncontrollably. His girlfriend was sitting on top of him. His body was moving so rapidly that I thought the film had speeded up. Then I realized that he would go into spasm to get his girlfriend excited.

There was no explanation of what we were seeing or what we were supposed to be learning.

After the first couple was finished, a married couple with cerebral palsy appeared. An attendant brought them into the room, undressed them, threw them onto the bed together, and then left the room. They had enormous difficulty getting close enough to each other to touch, so having sex took a very long time.

I was glad that John had not come. I knew that my accident would not affect our love or sex life in any significant way, and that to have watched this movie would not have helped us.

At first I thought that only the women didn't like the movie. But as the movie ended, we sensed the men didn't like it either. Everyone seemed embarrassed, and some had their heads down. A few had tears in their eyes. One by one, we silently wheeled out of the room. I didn't know whether they were sad because they realized how difficult it would be to have sex from now on, or whether they were uncomfortable with what they had seen.

Later, when we discussed it, we felt that the entire sex issue had been handled in a very inappropriate way.

At our next meeting with Evelyn, she said she had heard a lot of negative talk about the movie and asked for a show of hands of how many people had liked it. Only one middle-aged man raised his hand. Most of the men were in their twenties.

"I can't believe the rest of you didn't like it," Evelyn said. "I thought it was very educational. Would anyone tell me why they didn't like it?"

Art said, "I thought it was humiliating."

"Would you like to elaborate on that?" Evelyn asked.

"It made me sick to my stomach to think of me looking like that," Art said. "I can't see me turning on any girl the way I am now. I've always been a macho guy. I'm the one who chopped the wood and carried it into the house. I always started the fire in the fireplace. The thought of a girl doing everything for me freaks me out."

There were no other comments. I could tell by the looks on their faces, that most of the guys in the room felt what Art was feeling.

Evelyn was insulted by our response. She told us she had shown the movie to several patients in a Missouri hospital and they had enjoyed it and thought it was beneficial. She dismissed class early.

26

Mary

One day I overheard two nurses talking about a patient named Mary, and how difficult it was to be assigned to her room. She was unhappy, seldom talked to anyone, and didn't like the nurses. I wanted to meet her, so I asked what room she was in. I decided I would visit her after my last class of the day. I wasn't sure what I would say to her. If I told her I had a strong desire to see her, she'd think I was crazy. I decided I would just go in and introduce myself. If she didn't want to talk, I wouldn't push.

When my last class was over, I wheeled to Mary's room. As I entered the room, I saw three young men and one woman, each in bed and barely able to move. Each was attached to a respirator. I asked the nurse if the woman sitting up in bed was Mary. She said it was. I wheeled to Mary's bed. She was pretty and nicely dressed in a yellow pants and top outfit.

"Hi, my name is Beverly. I just heard there was another woman on our ward besides me and my roommates. With so many men on the ward, I thought we gals should stick together."

I realized how stupid I sounded. I was searching for the right words to say and kept stumbling from one sentence to the next. I watched Mary's eyes as I talked. I could tell she didn't know why I was rambling on or why I was there. I couldn't remember everything I said to her, which was a blessing.

"I'd better be going, Mary. I hope you didn't mind me stopping by."

"No," she whispered.

"I would like to visit you everyday, but if you don't want me around, just say so. I won't bother you."

"I'd like you to visit," whispered Mary.

She couldn't speak louder because of her tracheostomy.

"Great," I said. "I'll see you tomorrow."

When I left, Mary's nurse followed me out in the hall and said, "I'm glad you came to visit Mary. Her family doesn't live in this area and she has few visitors. She usually doesn't talk to anyone, but she seems to have accepted you. We nurses can't seem to get close to her."

I wanted to say, "Maybe it's because you can't feel what it's like to be in her shoes," but I just smiled and told the nurse I would visit Mary every day.

After several visits, we became good friends. She told me about her accident. She had been vacationing in Yosemite and had rented a bicycle. As she gained momentum going downhill, she realized the brakes didn't work. She went off a cliff some thirty feet in the air and landed on her neck. She was totally paralyzed from the neck down. She had been at Valley for three years. After we exchanged stories, we both cried.

"I don't want to live anymore," cried Mary. "I'm tired of being imprisoned in my body. I can't get anyone to pull the plug for me. I want to die."

"I don't blame you, Mary. I've had the same feelings at times since my accident, and I'm only half as bad off as you. You were dealt a shitty hand."

"So were you, Bev. You don't deserve this."

"I have to believe that there is a good reason for all this,

Mary. Maybe someday God will show us. But for now I have to rely on faith."

"I know," she said. "Only, it's so unfair."

We cried some more. Our friendship was sealed.

I visited Mary as often as I could.

27

Roommates

The unhappiest patient on the ward was Flo. She gave the doctors and nurses a bad time. I felt sorry for her. I tried to talk with her and cheer her up as much as I could, but she just stared out the window. One day I heard her doctor tell her that there was nothing more they could do for her at the hospital. She was going to be sent to a nursing home. Flo wanted her children and mother to take her. The doctor told her he had talked with them, and they were unable to take her in.

The next day a nurse began packing Flo's belongings.

I said, "I'm sorry you're leaving us, Flo. We're going to miss you."

She began to cry and replied, "They're making me leave, and I don't want to go."

"Maybe it'll be better for you."

"Are you kidding? A nursing home is a place to die. Maybe that won't be bad after all. I'm tired of living."

"Don't talk like that, Flo. You have your family."

"My family doesn't want me, and I can't blame them. I haven't treated them very kindly."

Flo turned away to face the window. She didn't want to talk anymore. As I left the room, I said good-bye to her. When I returned, she was gone.

Over a week later, one of the nurses received a letter from Flo's nursing home and read the letter to us. Flo had died. I remember her saying, "A nursing home is a place to die." I felt that's what she had wanted. May she rest in peace.

Flo's bed had been taken by a new patient, a young man with a broken neck. At first we felt uneasy about sharing our room with a man, but in a short time we didn't mind. Stan was nice and had a pretty wife who often visited him.

Their story was sad. They had been away from home for the weekend, and Stan had been swimming in a river. When he dove underwater, he hit his head on something and broke his neck. Someone noticed him floating face down in the water and pulled him to shore. Others tried to find a doctor or nurse. His wife, a nurse, volunteered to help, not knowing that it was Stan. She was shocked to discover that the injured man was her husband. She gave him mouth-to-mouth resuscitation and revived him.

His medical insurance only covered injuries on the job. Stan and his wife wanted him in Valley Medical Center, because they had heard it was best for spinal cord injuries. Before Valley would accept him, Stan had to pay a large amount in advance, which took all their savings. They had asked family and friends for enough money to keep Stan in the hospital.

One day, several of his buddies came to visit Stan in the hospital. He seemed to have a pleasant time with them. When they left, he didn't realize I was in the room and began to cry. His shoulders were shaking and his head was down. I wanted to go to him and put my arms around him. I felt he must be thinking, "Why me?"

At first it's hard to be with old friends. It reminds you of the good times you had with them. You can never function the same way again. You cannot walk as they do. Many of the recent events they eagerly tell you about, you will never experience. It's hard to be satisfied with the limited number of things you can do. It's hard not to feel sorry for yourself and ask, "Why me?" For you, life will never again be easy.

As days passed, we adjusted to Stan, and Stan to us. I was lucky to have such a good group in my room.

28

The Nurses

The worst time for all the patients was during the graveyard shift from 11 PM-7 AM. Most of the nurses on that shift were inconsiderate. Their main chore was to turn patients every two hours, to prevent bedsores. We were lucky if we were turned every four hours.

One afternoon, the head nurse met with several of us to ask how we were doing and if we were getting satisfactory care. She seemed nice and truly concerned. She asked if we had any complaints. We all looked at each other, wondering if we should tell her what we thought of the night nurses.

Stan was the brave one and told her of some of his experiences.

"Sometimes they only turn me once during the night, and when they do, they're quite rough."

"That's awful," replied the nurse. "Why don't you tell them to turn you more often?"

"I can't always ring for them because I'm unable to reach the button if it isn't next to my hand. They don't come in our room often enough for me to ask."

"Why haven't you reported them to the head nurse on duty that night or to your doctor?"

"I don't want them mad at me," he said. "If I say anything, I'm afraid they'll treat me even worse. I try to be as polite to them as I can. Even when I ask for a sip of water, it's always, 'Please' and 'Thank you.' I'm afraid to make waves. Not being able to move makes me very vulnerable."

I looked at Stan and felt very sad. Here was this six foot, tough-looking guy, who, under normal circumstances, would have kicked butt if he was treated badly. Now, he's afraid to ask for a sip of water. I too felt vulnerable, but at least I could reach for a glass of water. As I looked around the room, I realized how fortunate I was.

I could tell the nurse was shocked. I decided to throw in my two cents. I told her about the following three incidents:

1) One night after I had been on the same side for over two hours, my shoulder began to hurt. Two nurses came in to turn Sandy. As they were leaving, I asked if I could be turned. They just looked at me and told me it wasn't time.

"It's been over two hours, and my shoulder is hurting," I pleaded.

"We'll be back in an hour or so. Then we'll turn you. It hasn't been two hours yet."

I was so angry, I told them to forget it. I tried desperately to turn myself. I could twist my top half to the other side, but I couldn't budge the bottom half. With all the straining and grunting I was doing, I should have been able to move the entire bed. Instead, I ended up in a worse position, on my back and on my bedsore. I was so frustrated I wanted to scream. Now I had to ring for a nurse. She wouldn't like it, but I knew I wasn't supposed to lie on my bedsore. If I had been turned when I had asked, she wouldn't have had to make an extra trip. When a nurse arrived, I was happy to see it wasn't one of the previous two. This nurse didn't complain and quietly moved me off my back and onto my other side. I decided not to complain. Like the other patients, I was afraid of what the graveyard nurses would do if I complained.

2) Another time when I needed to be turned, a very large nurse scooped me up and literally threw me on my side. I was afraid she had damaged my back.

3) About 2 AM one morning Charley, a GU tech, woke me to tell me he was sorry that he had spilled a container of urine on my bed. He assured me that he had told the nurse about it, and she had said she would change my sheets. Unfortunately, I had taken a sleeping pill and again fell asleep. At 6 A.M. a nurse came in to clean my bedsore and noticed my bed was wet.

I tried to mimic in a funny voice what the nurse had said to me, "My, my, looks like you had an accident in bed."

The head nurse interrupted my story with a question, "Are you sure the tech told the nurse?"

"Oh, I'm sure. Why would Charley wake me up? He could have said nothing, and I would have believed the nurse."

"Did you tell the nurse what Charley had told you?"

"I sure did. I was so angry. I was covered with urine and my bedsore was soaked."

"What did she say when you told her?"

"Nothing. She cleaned me up, changed my bedsore dressing, changed the bed, and left."

By the time everyone had told their story, an hour had passed. The nurse stood up and said, "I'm going to talk with the doctors about this and see what can be done. I promise I won't give out names."

We saw some change in the night nurses. They were quieter when they came into our room. They even seemed nicer. We hoped it would last.

I was adjusting to the hospital and my therapy. I was close to the patients in our ward. We were like one big family. We were each other's support and looked out for one another.

One night we had a new nurse in our room. Whenever a new nurse appeared in our room, we watched her carefully. It didn't take us long to rate a nurse. If they were fair to awful, we had to watch out for each other.

This nurse was bad. She had to transfer Cathy from one wheelchair to another and was going to try to do it alone. We all knew it took two people to do the transfer. Sandy and I both mentioned she should get help. Apparently she wanted to show us she didn't need help. Cathy was a moderately heavy quad and was wearing a twelve pound halo, which makes a patient top heavy.

Cathy was scared. We held our breath as the nurse bent down in front of Cathy and draped Cathy's upper half over her shoulder. It didn't look good. As the nurse tried to lift her, Cathy started to slide to the floor. Sandy and I yelled for help. In a few seconds there were three nurses in the room, just in time to save Cathy from a serious fall. Cathy smiled and thanked us. We knew how important it was to watch out for each other. In our room I was the most mobile and tried to help the others as much as I could. It felt good to be useful again.

29

The Mirror

Things were going smoothly for me, except for the pain. Some days were better than others. I would try to take advantage of those days, by doing as much therapy as I could. When the pain was bad, I was useless. But, all in all, I was doing as well as expected. My physical and occupational therapy were progressing. I was pretty good at dressing myself. Although I couldn't put my shoes on, I could put on my pants with the help of the hook.

Most of us looked forward to Sunday, the only day we didn't have to work. After the doctor's 9 A.M. rounds, we were free.

I'll never forget one Sunday morning. The doctor making rounds was not my doctor, but Sandy's and Cathy's doctor and also the head of the department. He came in with several residents. He was hard on his patients, and I was glad he wasn't my doctor.

When Sandy had first wiggled a toe, she was so excited that she couldn't wait to tell her doctor. He wasn't impressed. He told her not to bother him until she could move her whole leg. We couldn't believe what he had said.

Unfortunately for me, this morning he was checking everyone. I was apprehensive.

When he reached my bed, he said, "So you're the one with the bedsore."

In the past, I had been recognized for my tennis, my art

work, my dancing, or as John's wife, but never for my bedsore.

I knew my bedsore was large from comments the nurses made when they changed the dressing. To get this much recognition, it must be the talk of the hospital. I could tell he couldn't wait to feast his eyes on it. They rolled me on my side and removed the dressing.

"Have you seen your bedsore?" he asked.

"No," I replied.

His presence made me uneasy, and his question made me more anxious.

"Well, then," he said, "we'll have to fix that. Do you have a mirror?"

"No, I don't," I replied, hoping that would be the end of it.

"Nurse, get me a mirror."

"Really, doctor, I don't want to see it. It will only make me sick."

"Nonsense, I want you to look at it."

The nurse handed him the mirror, and he adjusted it so I could see my bedsore if I turned my head.

"Come on now," he insisted, "turn your head."

By the tone of his voice, I knew there was no way out. I didn't know what to expect. I didn't have any feeling there. I knew it wasn't going to be pretty. As I looked in the mirror, it took me a few seconds to make out what I was looking at. It was the ugliest thing I had ever seen. It was about four inches across and round, like the rim of a glass. The flesh looked like it had been eaten away. I could actually see some bone.

"Oh my God," I screamed.

I was horrified and began to cry.

The doctor didn't say a word to me. He calmly told the

145

nurse to put a new dressing on it, and then he left.

The nurse came over and put her arms around me.

"That was uncalled for," she said. "I don't know what good it does for you to see your bedsore."

I was very upset at what I had seen, but angrier with the doctor for forcing me to look at it.

That evening I told John what had happened. He felt bad and tried to console me. I began feeling better. Being with loved ones always brightened my day.

That night, after everyone left, I thought about what had happened that day. I was wasting valuable energy with useless anger. It was time to take control. I knew I couldn't make the bedsore disappear overnight, but I could help with the healing process. I'd read about positive thinking and visualization for healing. After I had learned self-hypnosis, I used it to help heal some of my minor injuries. I was amazed at the effect it had. I knew this wasn't a minor injury, but now was a good time to try again. Now that I had seen the sore, I could visualize it shrinking every day. It would take a lot of concentration.

"I wonder if I'm up to it?" I thought. "That's negative thinking. No more negative thoughts. I WILL be able to concentrate. I WILL be able to heal my bedsore."

As I tried to think positively, another thought came to mind, "Vitamins!"

I'd taken vitamins for years, and since I'd been in the hospital, I hadn't had any. The next day I'd ask my doctor to prescribe vitamins B and C, iron, and zinc. The B vitamins are good for stress, and God knows I'd had my share. I felt I needed 'C' because I hadn't eaten properly, and zinc is a must for healing. I needed iron because I had lost so much blood, and they were drawing blood from me every day.

30

In a Car Again

Monday morning I started another day as usual: washing, brushing my teeth, and getting dressed for breakfast. It sounds easy, but accomplishing this in bed without half of your body working is quite a feat. I started at seven-thirty and finished by nine, just before doctor's rounds. I talked to the doctor about my taking vitamins and minerals. He said it was a good idea.

Donna arrived and said, "Hi, Bev. Today we will do something different. Since you've been doing so well transferring on your sliding board from bed to chair, I want you to practice transferring into a car."

"Okay," I said.

She walked alongside my chair telling me where to go. (No one pushed anyone in a wheelchair. That's a no-no.) She directed me to the parking lot in front of the hospital, where there was a large, old, two-door automobile. As we approached the car, my stomach felt strange and I didn't know why. By the time we reached the car, I felt worse.

Donna opened the door for me on the passenger side.

"This is more difficult than transferring from chair to bed because the distance is greater," said Donna. "It will be hard for you at first, but like everything else, with practice, it'll get easier."

I thought about how easy it had been to get into a car and how I had taken it for granted. Now, with so much dead

147

weight from the waist down, it would be difficult and exhausting.

Donna gave me instructions on how to angle my chair, place the slide board, and position my hands. I did that without any problem. The hard part was putting my weight on my feet and legs, where I had no feeling, and then lifting my behind off the sliding board and onto the car seat. The whole movement felt so awkward, that I was frightened. I thought I would fall forward when I tried to lift and slide my body. The car door prevented me from getting my chair close to the car seat, so I had to lift and slide several times. It was very difficult, but my determination won out. For the first time since the accident, I was sitting in a car.

When the frustration wore off and my breathing slowed down, fear began to overwhelm me. My body shook and I broke out in a cold sweat. I was having trouble breathing. I hated being there. I wanted to jump out of the car and run. I felt trapped, just as I had been trapped in the car after the accident. I began to sob. Donna didn't say anything. She knew what I was going through. She waited till I calmed down. I pulled myself together and quietly struggled back into my chair. Neither of us spoke as we returned to my room.

31

Standing

My tilttable therapy didn't take much effort now that I was accustomed to being upright. Of course it wasn't the same as standing on my own. When I reported to Jill in the gym she said she had a surprise for me. She thought I was ready to use the standing frame. The standing frame consisted of a plywood platform with a steel post at each of the four corners. The posts were about four feet high, with a U-shaped bar lying on top of the posts.

Jill had me wheel in front of the frame. Two of my doctors were there to help and watch how I did. Jill told me where to place my hands on the frame, and then told me to pull myself up. The three of them surrounded me, and with much help, I reached a standing position. They strapped me to the frame.

That was one of my most memorable moments. It had been three months since I had been able to stand with all my weight on my feet. With Jill and the doctors beside me, everyone in the gym clapped for me. That was a big accomplishment for me. I was anxious to tell my family about it.

I had forgotten what it was like to be at eye level with people. I hated looking up from my chair; it was hard on my neck. I looked at Jill and asked if I was standing on a high platform.

"No, not really, just a piece of plywood about 1/4 inch thick."

I looked at my doctors and Jill and said, "Boy, you guys aren't very tall."

There was a surprised look on their faces, and they laughed. At 5'6" I was looking down at 5'2" Jill. The doctors were only a few inches taller than I. I hadn't realized that looking up from a chair made everyone seem taller than they really were.

*With my parents,
Al and Julie Crudo*

*My sons, Ken
and Gary*

*With Nono on his
75th birthday*

With my husband, John

Gary, his wife, Stephanie, and their children,
Samantha and Tony

*Ken with his
wife, Jyl*

*John's Daughter, Joan
her husband, Jim, and
their daughter, Alice*

John's Daughter, Amy

John and I receiving tennis trophies

With my favorite companions, Troy and Nike

With my new companion, Mandy

With my tennis partner, Nancy, after winning a tennis tournament

With longtime friend Gerry Carter

With my talented friend, Lynn, at a talent show rehearsal at Foothills Tennis Club

With Betty in Egypt

*Bev as Wonder Woman and
Gordie as Superman*

*Bev as Jerry Lewis doing
the* Typewriter Song

Bev as Cher

Bev as Liza

Some of the paintings I did after the accident

Flowers

Indian Girl

Still Life

The accident

Gerry Andrews and Sharon McCluskey, who died in the crash

Dee Siehl, who survived

32

The Kidney Test

Something new or unusual happened frequently. That night, as usual, I was handed my medication with dinner. Usually, I just put the pills in my mouth and swallowed. But I noticed the pills were different from the ones I usually took. I asked the nurse if my medication had been changed. When she looked at them, she realized she had given me Sandy's pills by mistake. Fortunately, I had noticed.

One day I was scheduled for a kidney test. Nurses transferred me to a gurney and wheeled me to an elevator. We went up several floors and got off. The nurses told someone that I was there and then left me alone in the hallway. I didn't know what was going to happen or when. After about half an hour, a nurse came out to ask me for the umpteenth time all the usual medical questions, such as my age, what childhood diseases had I had, and so on. Medical personnel often don't bother to look in the chart for needed information. It was another half hour before I was wheeled into a room. A doctor introduced herself. She filled a syringe full of fluid, telling me at the same time what she planned to do.

As she was about to stick me with the needle, I blurted out, "By the way, I have only one kidney."

I don't know why I said that. It came out as if someone were speaking for me. I didn't realize how important that statement was.

The doctor immediately stopped and looked at the nurse.

"That's great," she said, glaring at the nurse. "That's the first thing you ask a patient when you're doing this test. It's one of the first questions on that form you filled out. I was about to give this patient enough dye for two kidneys. That could have created problems!"

"I'm sorry," said the red-faced nurse.

The doctor removed half the dye from the syringe and injected the remaining fluid. She told me about the remainder of the test and that it would be painless.

"Thank God for that," I thought. "More pain I don't need."

The doctor pointed out the image of my kidney on a nearby screen.

"In a minute, we'll be able to see the dye as it reaches the kidney. The diuretic in the injected fluid will make this happen quickly. Then I will be able to see how well your kidney functions."

She pointed out what was taking place on the monitor and assured me all was going well. I was thrilled that my only kidney was working.

"That's it," she said. "You passed with flying colors. I'll call your nurse downstairs and tell her you're ready to leave."

The procedure took about an hour and a half, not counting the waiting time in the hall. I wondered how many hours I'd spent waiting since I'd been in the hospital.

While the nurse was on the phone, I became aware of my bladder for the first time since the accident. When I placed my hand over my bladder, it felt swollen. When the doctor returned, I told her what I was feeling.

"Is it possible my bladder is full, or am I imagining it?"

"It could be full from the diuretic."

She placed her hand on my bladder and said that it was full.

"Do you think you could wait to be cathed till you got back to your room?"

"I don't think so. It's starting to hurt."

"I'll call for a GU tech right away."

Kate and Brenda, my nurses from downstairs came in the room, thinking I was ready to leave. The doctor told them what was happening and asked them to wait till the tech arrived.

"Can you tell them to hurry? It's really getting painful," I cried.

"I'll call again and tell them it's a STAT."

I thought my bladder would burst. It seemed forever for the GU tech to show up. The doctor asked my nurses if they would move me into the hall to wait for the tech. She had to use the room for another patient.

"That's great," I thought. "Nothing like having to be cathed in front of God and the world."

Kate must have known what I was thinking.

"Don't worry, Bev, we'll find an empty room for you."

I heard the elevator doors open, and the familiar sound of the tech's cart. I could tell it was moving quickly by the noise it made and the rapid footsteps that followed. As it approached, I saw Charley, the GU tech, coming to the rescue. Kate and Brenda immediately started to look for an empty room.

"Over here," said Brenda. "This room is empty."

They rushed me inside and Charley followed. It was a lab room, with long counter tops, sinks, and microscopes. I didn't care what room it was, as long as there were no nonprofessional people in it.

"Charley, I can't tell you how happy I am to see you!"

Even though I knew he was moving as quickly as he could, it seemed like slow motion. I had so much urine that I was filling up the pan, and Charley asked Kate to get another pan from his cart. I finally passed 900 cc of urine (400 to 600 cc is normal maximum capacity).

"Me and my bladder thank you, Charley. You saved my life."

"Any time," he said.

33

Exercise Classes

By the time I returned to my room, I was tired enough to stay in bed the rest of the day. I looked at the clock and realized that, if I hurried, I could make my weightlifting class. I didn't want to miss any therapy, especially with Dave, my favorite physical therapist. He worked us hard and made sure we were getting the most from our exercises. He took our minds off the strenuous exercises with his singing, story telling, and corny jokes.

As I wheeled inside the gym, I saw Dave, surrounded by my classmates. They had already selected weights and were in a circle, ready to begin the exercises.

"You're late!" shouted Dave with a twinkle in his eye. "You'll have to use twenty-pound weights today."

"I'm wheeling as fast as I can," I replied with a smile.

"You should be able to go faster than that. I better give you more exercises to do."

He loved to tease, and we all loved it. I was doing well in the class. I was lifting six pounds in each hand. I was able to do all the exercises and several repetitions in each exercise.

When I wheeled over to the box of weights to select some, Dave informed me that I wouldn't need them any more.

"You'll be glad to know you've graduated to the pulleys," he said.

I wasn't glad. I would miss Dave and his class. Dave walked with me to the other side of the gym. He introduced me to my new therapist, who was pretty and had a nice smile. After Dave left, she motioned to me to turn my chair around and back up to the marks on the floor. Then she handed me two pulleys. When she didn't give me instructions, I turned to see her looking at the wall charts. I asked her what I should do next. She smiled. As she spoke, I realized she couldn't speak English well, and I couldn't understand what she was saying. She obviously didn't know much about the pulleys.

I was so angry, I let go of the pulleys, and they fell to the floor with a crash.

"Forget it," I yelled. "I'll work with free weights on my own."

The whole gym became quiet.

I wheeled to the other side of the gym and picked up some small weights. The head therapist came over and asked what was wrong.

"I can't believe you have someone teach a class who can't speak English."

"Calm down," she said. "She can speak some English. This is her first day on the job and she has to learn how things work."

"Shouldn't she be working with another therapist until she does learn?"

"We're short of therapists right now. She was a therapist in Portugal before she came here. As soon as she can read and write English, she can take the test to receive her California license as a physical therapist."

"I'm sorry I got upset, but I don't have many weeks left till I go home. To me it's very important that I get quality therapy time. I don't mean to hurt her feelings, but I want another therapist to work with me on the pulleys."

"I'll talk to your doctor about it and see what he suggests."

I was exhausted. The kidney test, my overdistended bladder, losing my favorite PT, wasting twenty minutes of valuable therapy time because a new PT couldn't read the directions, combined with my leg and foot pain, were too much. It was only two o'clock. I barely got through my next two classes.

I decided to skip my last class, a lecture on bladder care. I couldn't care less. I was exhausted. All I wanted to do was rest. I returned to my room.

34

Ben

As I was about to doze, a man in his late twenties wheeled up to my bed.

"Are you Bev Differding?"

"Yes, that's me."

"My name is Ben, and we have a mutual friend."

"Who might that be?"

"Lori Turner. She sent me to talk to you. She thought I could give you some helpful ideas on what can be done in a wheelchair. I've been a quad for fifteen years, and I can get around pretty well. Last week I was in a wheelchair race."

As he talked, I was trying to figure out who the hell Lori Turner was.

"Did you say Lori Turner?"

"That's right. She belongs to the same tennis club you do."

Then it dawned on me. I had said "Hi" to her a few times, but I hardly knew her. I didn't tell Ben that. He told me all the wonderful things I could do after I left the hospital. I knew he meant well, and I knew Lori thought she was doing me a favor by sending Ben. But now was not the right time. The more he talked about wheelchair sports, the more I resented him. I had all I could do to survive. I hated talk about doing things from a chair. I considered it negative. I didn't plan to spend the rest of my life in a wheelchair.

I tried to be polite, but it wasn't easy.

It was surprising how many people thought they knew what was best for me. It would have been nice if Lori had called me before sending Ben to see me. I continued to smile and nod my head. The final aggravation was when he whipped out a magazine about wheelchair tennis.

"Since you're a tennis player," he said, "I thought you might like to look through this magazine."

"What I would like to do with this magazine," I thought, "is roll it up and beat you over the head with it."

Instead, I thanked him and told him I didn't have time to read it now.

"That's all right," he said, "I'll leave it with you and pick it up in a couple of weeks."

When he left, I placed the magazine on a shelf by my bed where no one would notice it. If John saw it, he might try to convince me that it would be fun to do. I knew he meant well, but I wanted to get strong enough to walk.

Thinking positively about walking again was difficult, especially when no one else thought I would. People who talked to me about doing things from a wheelchair were telling me that they were convinced that I would never walk. I guess they thought once a paraplegic, always a paraplegic. The important thing was I KNEW I was going to walk.

35

A Fun Weekend

On Saturday the hospital had a barbeque for the patients and their families on the lawn in front of the hospital. I enjoyed being outside. John shared the day with me. I don't know what I would have done without John. He brightened my day.

On Sunday, John had a surprise for me. He wheeled me outside on the front lawn of the hospital and told me he would be right back. He returned with Nike, my shepherd-husky who was ten years old and didn't see too well. I was excited to see her and called her name. She didn't recognize me in the wheelchair and approached cautiously. I thought that it'd been so long since she'd seen me that she didn't know who I was. When she finally got a good whiff of me, she excitedly ran around my chair, moaning and squeaking. She tried to jump up in my lap, but she was too big to fit. She licked my face, and I began to cry.

"She still remembers me."

"Of course she does," replied John.

It was my best weekend since the accident. I wished I could have seen my other dog, Troy, a Great Dane mix. But it was too hard for John to bring both dogs. I was pleased. I realized how much I missed being home.

36

Panic

Monday morning, I checked the bulletin board to see what adventures they had in store for me for the week. At 2 PM I was scheduled for a bladder test. I decided not to get upset. There was nothing I could do about it.

After my morning classes, my friend Lynn brought lunch. I appreciated her visits. She was always warm, enthusiastic, and friendly.

Finally, it was time to go for my test. Nurses transferred me onto a gurney.

"How long do you think this test will take?" I asked.

"I'm not sure," said Kate. "I wouldn't think it would be too long, but it's hard to say."

Two nurses wheeled me to the elevator. We went down to the basement to the Radiology Department. I was parked in the hall. Kate went inside to tell them I was waiting.

When she returned, she said, "They'll be ready for you in a few minutes." (I've heard that before. It may be the most common medical joke.) "When they finish your test, they'll call us to come and pick you up." Then the nurses left.

I waited over an hour, uncomfortable and alone. If it weren't for the wall clock, I would have sworn I'd waited three hours. Radiology personnel went in and out the door many times. No one spoke to me or even looked at me. They acted like I wasn't there. Finally, a radiology tech came out, and without a word, pushed my gurney inside. I expected an apology for my long wait, but no, I was just another body to be X-rayed.

The room was so small that two techs had a tough time moving the gurney next to the X-ray table so they could transfer me. The techs and the woman doctor looked like they had been sucking lemons. I wondered if they always looked liked that or if they were having a bad day. As they prepared for the procedure, one discovered that my ostomy bag was leaking.

"We can't continue till we get this fixed," said the doctor. "It will contaminate everything."

One tech said, "I'll call the nurse upstairs and ask her to bring down supplies to change the ostomy bag."

I asked, "Can't you put a washcloth or something over it? I just want to get out of here."

"You're not the only one who wants to get out of here," said the nasty tech.

I couldn't restrain myself.

"At least you have two legs that work so you can go home. I'm stuck here."

"Go make the call," snarled the doctor at the tech. Then she turned to me and said, "I'm sorry, Mrs. Differding, this shouldn't take too long once we get started."

I was upset with the nasty tech, the uncomfortable narrow hard table, and my leaking bag.

Soon my nurse came in with my supplies. She cleaned me up and replaced the bag. She gave me a smile and said she'd see me upstairs. I appreciated the smile. This room was as gloomy as its inhabitants, the lemon sisters.

The doctor told me they were going to test my bladder function but didn't tell me what they were going to do to me. When the test was finally over, she told the tech to finish up and walked out of the room. I wasn't thrilled to be alone with this tech. She didn't like me, and I felt very vulnerable.

A few minutes after the doctor left, she said, "It's time for my break. I'll send someone in to take care of you."

Before I could reply, she was out the door.

As I lay on my back, I looked around the room. I was alone and claustrophobic. I tried to calm myself, saying that any second someone would come through the door. The room was so small. There were no windows. Above me was a large X-ray machine. The table I was on was so narrow I couldn't put my arms at my sides and had to fold them over my chest. I didn't have my back brace on, so I couldn't sit up. I wanted to turn on my side so I wouldn't damage my bedsore, but I was afraid that if I moved at all, I'd fall off the table. Minutes passed, and still no one came. I had difficulty breathing. I wanted to escape.

"Oh, how I wish I could walk," I thought. "I'm helpless. My God, if someone doesn't come soon, I'm going to scream." Tears filled my eyes.

"HELP ME," I screamed. "PLEASE, SOMEBODY HELP ME. HELP!"

I was hysterical. I had never lost control before. I kept screaming for help, hardly taking a breath. I was getting hoarse. Tears were streaming down my face. My body was shaking. I couldn't stop screaming. I wasn't sure anybody could hear me.

It seemed like a hell of a long time before a male tech came in. He tried to calm me down. I stopped screaming. I remember how soft and calm his voice was. It took some time for me to stop sobbing and shaking. He kept reassuring me while he called to have one of my nurses come to pick me up. I heard him say over the phone that he couldn't leave me. When Kate and Brenda arrived, they put me on the gurney and took me to my room. I was so exhausted all I wanted to do was sleep.

I didn't want any more tests, but I was told that all patients in rehab had to pass tests in physical therapy and occupational therapy before they could be released from the hospital.

37

Outside

I knew I would be going home soon. Some patients talked mostly about going home and getting out of this awful place. Some of my friends had received their discharge date and celebrated. They seemed happy till the day arrived when they had to leave. That seemed strange, but I thought it was because they hated to say good-bye to all their friends. I was anxious to go home.

The day arrived when I was to be tested in occupational therapy. I had no idea what I would have to do. I thought I had learned it all. I could dress myself, except for my shoes. I couldn't bend my legs and back enough so that my hands could reach my feet. That wasn't critical. I could manage without shoes. I could transfer to a chair, a bed, a bathtub, or a car. They had taught me how to get around in a kitchen. What more could there be?

"Hi," said Donna, as she walked in the room. "Today we're going outside. You're going to wheel yourself around the outside of the hospital building, while I walk beside you. Are you ready?"

"I think I can handle that."

"Good. Let's go."

I was doing fine until I wheeled down a busy side street. People stared at me. I was embarrassed being in a wheelchair, and wearing my ugly thick plastic backbrace made it worse.

"No wonder people are staring at me," I thought.

I kept telling myself that it would be over soon. Donna walked beside me, talking up a storm and treating me as if nothing was wrong with me. My arms were tired, but I didn't say anything. I wanted to pass this test so I could go home. We had gone a long way. Just when I thought we were through, Donna pointed to the busy intersection at the end of the block.

"So she wants to see if I can cross the street," I thought. "I don't think that's a big deal."

Was I in for a shock. I wheeled to the corner. As we waited for the light to change, I was frightened. The noise of the cars turning the corner brought back memories of the crash. They seemed so close to me. I was aware of how close to the ground I was. I worried that drivers wouldn't see me. The swooshing sound of the cars, the horns honking, and the tires screeching were too much. I felt tears forming.

"You big baby," I thought. "It's no big deal, you can do it. Stop your stupid crying and get your buns across the street."

When the signal changed, I pushed my chair as fast as I could, to keep ahead of Donna, so she couldn't see my tears. I wasn't going to let her know I was upset. I reached the opposite sidewalk.

"Well, you did it, Bev," said Donna.

"Did you have any doubts?" I asked.

She smiled and said, "No, I didn't. Let's head back to the hospital."

I'd successfully completed another stressful day.

38

The Parallel Bars

The next morning I wheeled to the bulletin board, hoping for a day without tests. Don was checking his schedule. Suddenly, he let out a whoop.

"I'm going home in a week," he yelled.

He gave me a big smile.

"Congratulations," I said.

If anyone was ready to go home, it was Don. He was a 28-year-old ex-marine who had more guts and courage than anyone on the ward. When his tow-truck rolled over, he had broken his neck and had severe burns on his arms and hands. He had had multiple skin grafts. He had been told that he would never have much movement from the neck down. He had been in the hospital longer than most of us. As I got to know him, I knew he would do fine. He was tough and strong-minded. When I first met him, he told me he was going to walk out of the hospital without a wheelchair, braces, or crutches. He was about to reach his goal.

"We'll miss you, Don," I said.

"Don't look so sad; your name is up there too."

I focused on the board and saw my discharge date was September first, just two weeks away. I smiled, thinking how great it would be to see my home and dogs again. Four months is a long time to be in a hospital.

I thought about leaving rehab. I knew I'd miss my friends. Living here for two months had taught me much about life. I learned what it took to survive and, more important, what it took to live life to its fullest. I'd watched my friends, noting that some did much better than others and wondered why. I often compared Sandy and Don with other patients. Both had been badly injured, but they improved and others didn't. I concluded that it must be their positive attitude.

The idea that they would never walk didn't cross their minds. They were disciplined and determined. Don, who had been a marine, and Sandy, who had been a champion body builder, had developed those qualities before their accidents. Those qualities helped them overcome their tragedies.

I was anxious to tell my family that I would be coming home in two weeks. John was helping Mr. Scott, a carpenter who was a friend of my son Ken, put in ramps in the front and back of our home. I knew John was ready for me to come home. I had to stop daydreaming and go to therapy.

As I worked with Jill that morning, I told her I would be going home in two weeks.

"That's great, Bev," she said. "That means we must make the best of these next two weeks. Maybe it's time for you to try walking between the parallel bars. Do you think you're ready for that?"

"Am I. I've been waiting for this."

"Great, let's try it."

We went to the gym. I'd watched patients using the bars during my therapy classes and longed to use them too. Jill told me to wait by the bars, while she went to get some leg braces. I wheeled my chair to the end of the bars and faced them, eagerly awaiting the chance to stand and take a few steps. Jill returned with big, heavy-looking metal braces with big brown men's shoes on the ends. Jill laughed when she saw me in the ready position between the bars. She knelt in front of me, put the braces on me, and strapped them tightly to my legs. The braces were so long that they came up to my wahzoo. She asked if I was ready.

"You bet!"

She told me how to place my hands on the bars and pull myself to an upright position. I placed my hands as she said and tried to pull myself up. I couldn't get my fanny off the chair. The braces were locked at the knees and heavy as hell. I couldn't imagine anyone getting themselves out of a chair wearing them.

"You've got to be kidding," I said. "How do you expect me to lift myself up when my legs are straight out in front of me?"

"Calm down," she said. "I'll help you up till you get the hang of it."

Around my abdomen she placed a wide strap that had a handle on it. This would give her a better hold on me if I started to fall. The handle was just above my navel. Now my outfit was complete. If my friends could see me now. Jill grabbed the handle of the strap, and helped pull me up.

"Now," she asked, "how does that feel?"

"I feel like Frankenstein."

"Are you comfortable?"

She had to be kidding. I couldn't possibly be comfortable, but I said, "I'm okay."

She asked me to swing one foot forward and then the other. It wasn't as easy as I had thought it would be, but then nothing ever was. I had no feeling from the waist down, so I couldn't tell where my feet were. The braces were so damn heavy, that it was very difficult to swing my legs forward. My arms hurt greatly, because they had to support my entire weight plus the braces. I was only able to take three steps.

I wished I could have thought of something wonderful to say, like "one small step for man, one giant step for mankind." I couldn't think of anything original. Those three steps were harder than playing three sets of tennis. I gasped and sweat dripped in my eyes. I was glad I had taken my first three steps. I would have felt better if I hadn't had to struggle so.

"Okay, Bev, I'll wheel your chair behind you," Jill said.

I wanted to sit down. My arms were shaking. I started to fall. Jill held on to the handle of the strap around my middle and called to Dave. I was leaning backwards with my legs straight in front of me. The braces didn't allow me to bend my knees. Dave hurriedly wheeled my chair behind me and put on the brakes. They grabbed me under my arms and placed me in the chair. That was too close for comfort. Another adventure in the life of Beverly.

"Don't worry, Bev. We'll try it again soon. You still need to take your physical therapy test. I'll have Dave test you. I'll see if he has time to do it today."

"What will he test me on?"

"He'll see how well you can handle yourself in certain situations. You'll do fine."

39

The Final Test

I attended the rest of my classes, but continually thought about the upcoming test. Late in the afternoon, Dave found me in the hall talking with my friends.

"Come on, tiger," he said. "I'm going to give you the big test now."

I wheeled into the gym with Dave walking beside me. I asked what I had to do.

"First, I want you to crawl on your hands and knees all the way across this mat and back to me."

"I can't get on my hands and knees, Dave. I can't lift my buns off the ground."

"No problem, you can do the combat crawl."

I didn't know what that was, so Dave got on the mats and showed me. He crawled without using his legs, as I would have to do. He used only his elbows and shoulders to move his body across the mat. It didn't look that hard, but I had learned that no matter how easy anything looked, it would be a struggle for me.

I transferred to the mat from my chair and, with difficulty, rolled over on my stomach. I began to crawl. My thick plastic brace stuck to the mat and made it harder for me to move. Dave timed me as I crawled up and down on the mats. There were five mats, each about five feet wide, placed together. So I crawled about fifty feet, dragging my bottom half, which felt like a hundred pounds of dead weight.

"Why is this important for me to do?"

"If you fell out of your chair, we need to be sure that you could crawl to a phone to call for help."

The second thing I had to do was to lower my body two feet from the mat to the floor. I found it very difficult. I was frightened and couldn't bring myself to drop my body that far. I use the word drop, because that's how I felt I had to accomplish the task. Dave showed me several different ways I could lower myself. To me there seemed only one way I could get to the floor. I wasn't going to risk breaking any bones to pass a stupid test. Dave held me under the arms and gently sat me on the floor.

Next he wanted me to lift myself up onto the mat. He tried to get me to pull myself up many different ways, but I was unsuccessful. Dave decided I had tried enough. He told me I would be able to master these tasks in due time.

Next I was to wheel my chair a half mile as fast as I could go. Dave told me the circular route to take in the hospital corridors, which I was to repeat four times. He had me start in front of a mark on the floor. He pulled out his stopwatch and told me to go.

That was the first time I had to go that far at top speed. I wheeled as fast as I could, worrying about running into somebody. Apparently, most of the people who worked at the hospital knew about these races. When they saw me coming, they immediately pressed themselves against the wall. Some cheered me on. What a crazy place. Each time I passed Dave, he yelled out my time, told me how many laps I had left, and encouraged me. When I finished, my arms and hands were really sore. Dave gave me a pat on the back and told me I did great.

"What was my time?" I panted. (I can't believe how

competitive I am in everything I do.)

"Well, you didn't make it in twelve minutes, but thirteen-three isn't bad for a first time."

I felt good about my accomplishments. When I had arrived in rehab six weeks earlier, I couldn't sit in a chair, and now I'd wheeled half a mile in thirteen minutes and three seconds. I felt each success brought me closer to walking.

Some of us spent more time than usual with Don, because he was leaving soon. We were sad to be losing a close friend. When the morning arrived for Don to leave, he didn't seem as anxious to go home as he had been. He wasn't his usual tough self. As he said his good-byes, I watched his face.

"What's wrong, Don?" I asked. "You don't seem happy to be leaving."

"I've been in this hospital for so damn long, I'm not sure what's out there. I'm a little scared."

"Don't worry, Don, you'll do just fine."

We hugged each other. Then he turned around and, with only a cane to help him, walked out the door. I had a feeling that it wouldn't be long before he threw away the cane.

40

Leaving

Although I'd been hospitalized for four months, it felt more like four years. Hopefully, in a week I'd be leaving this place. I thought of my friends here and realized that I probably wouldn't see them again.

I was concerned about my quadriplegic friend Mary whom I visited regularly. Who would spend time with her after I left? I felt sad as I told her that I would be going home soon. She handled it well; she smiled and told me she was happy for me. I promised I would write and would keep praying for her. I wished I could have done more.

With so little therapy time left, I wanted to accomplish as much as I could. I worried about my almost constant pain. I could work through the dull pain, but not through the sharp stabbing pains I had in my legs and feet. The doctors tried not to give pain medication. But when I hurt so badly that I was crying and couldn't get out of bed for therapy, they gave me something for the pain. Most of the time I had to struggle through the pain.

Thursday night John came late to visit. He told me what was being done to the house so it would be ready for me. The hospital wouldn't release me until the ramps for the house were complete. Mr. Scott, a carpenter who took pride in his work, was installing ramps to the front and two back doors. He exceeded the specifications suggested by the hospital. John helped him every evening between five and nine and then came to see me at the hospital. John visited me every day.

Friday morning the plastic surgeon and his resident came for their weekly visit. He was impressed by how well my bedsore was healing. Today would be his last look.

"Beverly, I don't know what you're doing to heal the bedsore, but whatever it is, keep doing it."

"I'm eating better and taking vitamins."

Some doctors don't believe in visualization, so I didn't tell him that I was using it.

"Well, it's healing. You still have a way to go. A sore that size probably won't heal completely on its own, and you'll need a skin graft. It won't be difficult to have it done. There is a good plastic surgeon at the Clinic who can take care of it."

That was discouraging to hear. But I figured that if it's healing as well as he says, there's no reason I couldn't heal it completely. Visualization and good food with vitamins and minerals could do the job.

That afternoon I wheeled outside to sit in the sun. I wanted to be alone to think about going home. In just four days I would be discharged. What a mess I had been when I first came to Valley Medical Center. I had to lie straight, I couldn't sit up, and I couldn't bend my knees. In less than two months my progress had been impressive. I could dress myself and get around easily in a wheelchair. I was much stronger and had a positive attitude. Still, I couldn't move my legs. I had limited feeling from the waist down and none from the knees down.

I wanted to walk out of the hospital like Don had. But then he had been in Valley Medical Center for nine months.

I had misgivings about going home; I really didn't want to leave the hospital. Here I was safe. If something went wrong, doctors and nurses were close by. Therapists were available to help me improve. Other patients supported me and related to me. They understood what it was like to be in a wheelchair. In the hospital I wasn't different.

At home there would be no one like me. Everyone would stare at me, feel uncomfortable, feel sorry for me, and not know what to say.

I thought of the time when four of us had been taken to a nearby restaurant for lunch. I was embarrassed and self-conscious to be in public. I hated my paralysis, my back brace, my wheelchair, and especially my pain. I felt like a fish out of water. I didn't want to leave!

That night when John came, he sensed something was wrong.

"Only a few more days and you'll be home where you belong," he said.

"I don't belong home. I'm of no use to anybody. I'm a freak that people will stare at."

"What in the world are you talking about?"

"I'm scared. What if the house catches fire? I can't get up the hill to the street. What if someone breaks in? I can't run away."

"Babe, don't worry about getting to the street if there's a fire. There are ramps at every outside door so you'll be able to get to a safe place. As for someone breaking in, our dogs will protect you. The dogs and I have not been doing well without you home. The dogs are lonely during the day, and I'm lonely at home without you there."

That's what I needed to hear. I was feeling sorry for myself and I was frightened. Being paralyzed makes you feel so vulnerable. I decided I would never be a burden. At home I would take care of myself. I must think positively. It was surprising how often I forgot that. I held onto John's hand as we talked. By the time he left, I felt better. I did want to go home.

Discharge was near. Because I had no bladder function, I had to learn how to pass a catheter into my bladder. GU technicians had been working with me for more than a week, but I still found cathing difficult. They assured me that once I was home, I would find it easier. I hoped they were right. After all I'd been through, I didn't want to die of a ruptured bladder. I had one more day to work on it.

That afternoon my doctor gave me an envelope full of prescriptions that I was to fill at the hospital pharmacy before I went home. I was also to pick up a special dressing material for my bedsore. Fortunately, John knew how to take care of my bedsore. He would have to change the dressing every night until it healed, which the doctor thought might be three months. The nurse gave me a list of other things I needed to take home, such as ostomy supplies and catheter kits. Everything seemed to have been taken care of, except for packing my belongings. I would do that just before I was ready to leave.

I could tell my roommates were happy for me, but sad that I would be gone. I wrote down their phone numbers and addresses. I wanted to keep in touch.

John didn't stay long that night. He had many things to do before he came for me the next day. I was anxious. At last I would be going home.

The next day John arrived with empty boxes for my belongings. He put the packed boxes and my supplies in the car. It was time to say good-bye. For most of my friends, I had to be the one to give the hugs. We shed some tears and promised to write. The nurses wished me well. I saved my special friend Mary for last. I knew that would be the hardest good-bye. I wheeled into her room. I could tell she knew I was there, as she turned her eyes as far as she could toward the door.

"Hi, Mary," I said.

"Is it time for you to leave?" she whispered.

"Yes," I replied, as I wheeled close to her bed. I placed my hand over hers and then realized she couldn't feel my touch. I wanted her to know I cared. Touching can say so much more than words. Here was a beautiful woman in her early forties, and she couldn't feel a gentle touch.

"God damn it, Mary. It's just not fair."

I laid my head on her bed next to her hand and we both cried.

"I love you," she whispered.

"I love you too, Mary, and I'll write you often. I'll never forget you. God bless you."

John returned from loading the car.

"Have you said all your good-byes?"

"Yes."

"Well, let's head for home," he said happily.

Home

41

Home At Last

John wheeled me out of the hospital and to my car. He helped me transfer into my beautiful little red Honda. I could hardly hold back the tears. This was my car, the car I had used to run errands, to drive to tennis and golf matches, and, most enjoyable of all, to go shopping. I realized how much that that car meant to me and the freedom it gave me. Now I couldn't drive it. I could barely slide myself into the passenger's side without help. It was amazing how the simplest things had become so difficult for me.

John took the wheels off my chair and put them and the folded chair in the back seat. When he got in the car and started the motor, I felt tense. I knew the ride home was going to be difficult. I tried to keep calm by deep breathing. I didn't talk much. I was watching all the cars zooming by. This time I would be ready to warn John if it looked like we might have an accident. John kept asking if I was doing all right. I wished he would concentrate on his driving instead of worrying about me. I repeatedly answered that I was fine. He knew I was tense and in a lot of pain. The freeway traffic was heavy, and the drive seemed to take forever. As we got closer to home, I recognized the surroundings. I started to relax. When I saw our house, I sighed with relief. I had been away so long.

John parked the car in the garage and helped me into my chair. As he wheeled me toward the front door, he asked, "How do you like the ramps?"

"They're nice," I replied, although I hated them. Now anyone walking by would know that I was in a wheelchair. I disliked anything that reminded me I was in a wheelchair. I didn't tell John. He and Mr. Scott had worked hard to put them in, and John had just finished painting them. John opened the door and wheeled me inside. My dogs were happy to see me. They barked and licked my face. They couldn't get close enough to me. I began to cry. I had missed them too and was happy to be home with them again.

"Would you like to be wheeled through the house?" John asked.

"I'd like that. It's been a long time since I've been home."

"When your occupational therapist came to the house to see if it was ready for you to come home, she thought the ramps were great. However, she thought one of the bathroom doors was too narrow for you to get through easily. She suggested removing the door and the molding, and then hanging a curtain across the opening."

"That's ridiculous," I fumed. "That would look ugly. I'm not removing the door."

"Okay, Babe, I'm just telling you what she recommended."

I could get into every room. The bathrooms were difficult, but I managed. With a little practice, it would be a breeze.

"Babe, what about getting your folks or some friends to stay with you during the day, while I'm at work?"

"I don't need help. I can handle everything by myself," I said firmly.

Being dependent on so many people during my hospital stay had been very difficult for me. One doctor had suggested I have a nurse stay with me during the day. There was no way I would accept having a stranger take care of me in my house. I wanted to be independent. John and my folks were concerned about my being alone, but I assured them I could handle it.

My first day at home wasn't too difficult. I was able to catheterize myself without assistance. I would have had a great day if my leg pain hadn't been so bad. The doctors had told me that it was "good pain," indicating that nerves were regenerating. I'd been told that nerve regeneration could continue for up to four years. In most patients the pain eventually disappeared.

Since the accident, I had pain every day. Some days were better than others, but pain was always there. My legs and feet hurt. Sometimes the sensation was like pins and needles, as if I had been lying on them and they were asleep. Sometimes, I had a tightening feeling around my waist and down both legs, like muscle cramps. But when I felt the muscles, they weren't tight. Other times I had stabbing or shooting pains, like electric shocks. At times, I had all three at the same time. It seemed strange to have pain in a place where I had no feeling.

Many friends came to visit. My calendar was full. Sometimes, I was taken out to lunch. More frequently, people brought me lunch so they could visit me where I was comfortable. My friend Nancy organized a dinner schedule, Monday through Thursday for two months, with different people bringing dinner for John and me, so I didn't have to struggle to prepare dinner. It was a great idea. We saw friends and enjoyed excellent meals.

Since the accident, I seemed more aware of what

people were thinking and feeling. Most of my friends handled my injury well, but a few had a tough time being with me. If I noticed someone was uncomfortable, I tried to relax them by joking with them. I understood their discomfort. Sometimes it's hard to find the right words to say to someone who has been seriously injured. I knew I would have had a tough time if the tables were turned.

I thanked them for making the effort. It meant a great deal to me to know they cared. Sometimes, we didn't need to say much. To hold their hands, to see them smile, to have them acknowledge my pain, or to just have them there was often all that was needed.

I felt that bringing dinner to me made it easier for those friends who felt awkward with me. I always tried to be happy and not show them my pain, as I knew that would bother them. I knew how they felt and hoped they would be relaxed with me. It was great not to cook dinners. By evening, I was so exhausted from the pain that all I wanted to do was go to bed.

My pain was relentless and drained my energy. I hated to take pain pills. Sometimes, they didn't work, and other times they made me goofy. The thought of being dependent on drugs terrified me. I needed to be independent and in total control. My doctor at Valley Medical Center told me that addiction wouldn't be a problem as long as I only took drugs when I had pain. If I did that, I would be taking drugs every day. I decided to take them only if I was having company or going somewhere. John gets angry with me when he sees me in great pain and I haven't taken anything for it. We've had more arguments about that than anything else.

42

Therapy

When I left Valley Medical Center, I wasn't given instructions about further therapy. Once patients left the hospital, they were on their own. I suspect the doctors felt they had done all they could, and that you had accomplished all you could. I knew I would continue to improve.

I had been told that I should continue to wear my plastic vest whenever I sat up, but I disliked it intensely. It was difficult to put on, it was ugly, and it made me claustrophobic. I didn't believe I needed it. I seemed to do all right without wearing it, and finally I told John to throw it in the garbage can.

I needed to get organized. I wanted a therapist who would come to the house. John asked other doctors for recommendations for a physical therapist. Several suggested Diana. I called her and she agreed to see me.

The moment I met her, I knew we would make a good team. We decided she would come to the house three times a week to give me physical therapy. We looked for a place in the house where she could work with me. We couldn't work on the floor since I couldn't transfer to the floor easily. If I did, I couldn't get back in the wheelchair. In one room I had a large bed which was the right height for me to transfer to and from the wheelchair.

The next step was to get some equipment, so I could

exercise on my own. First, I needed a standing frame (an apparatus that I could be strapped into standing up) to improve my circulation. I wanted to stand for an hour without fainting, getting sick, or having to stop because of the pain. Second, I needed parallel bars, so I could practice balancing on my feet and swinging my legs as if I were walking. Third, I wanted something like bicycle pedals, that could be attached to a chair, so I could strengthen my legs.

John and I went to a firm that supplied equipment for the handicapped. We looked through their catalogs and ordered the equipment I needed. I waited anxiously for everything to be delivered.

Each day John strapped me into the standing frame, which consisted of two perpendicular bars that I could grasp with my hands, two knee supports in the front, and a strap that went around my fanny. In the front about elbow high was a flat tray that I could lean on or place something to read. We placed the standing frame in front of the TV set, so the time would pass more easily. Each day I tried to stand for half an hour or more.

After John helped me back into my wheelchair, I would transfer to the chair with the bicycle pedals. Since I had trouble balancing and couldn't move my lower legs or feet, it was very difficult for me to strap my feet to the pedals. My feet were floppy, and I had to be careful not to injure them. I had enough strength to push down the right pedal, but not enough to push down on the left one, so I couldn't make a complete circle with the pedals. It was frustrating.

I finally discovered a way to make them work. I placed a strap around my left foot and the pedal, so I could alternately pull on the strap with my hands and push down with my right leg. Because my anterior thigh muscles were strong, I could work the pedals in reverse, but it was months before I could push the pedals forward without the strap. Improvement was slow. Most irritating was that the more I pedaled, the greater the pain I had in my legs and feet. Once I was able to pedal forward, my goal was to pedal continuously for three minutes. When I reached that goal, I tried to increase the time. Eventually, I was able to pedal for thirty minutes. After that, I increased the tension on the pedals and slowly progressed from no tension to the seventh notch.

During this time, Diana came regularly and stretched my hips, legs, and feet. My muscles and joints were stiff. I needed more flexibility to stand.

I also asked Julie, a friend of mine who practices a form of acupressure called Jin Shin Jyutsu, if she would come to the house and give me treatments. She was delighted to help. She agreed to come once a week for as long as I wanted. Her treatments increased the energy flow throughout my body. They released some of the tension I felt and decreased the pain for a short time.

As time went on, I improved. I was able to slide down to the floor for my physical therapy. When I was done, I could get back on the sofa by myself and transfer to my chair. This was easier for both Diana and me.

However, it was hard to cope with the fact that the harder I worked, the more pain I had. Somedays I had to cancel my therapy. It was aggravating to lose time and sometimes to start over at a lower level. Improvements came slowly, making it hard to maintain a positive attitude. I knew I could do more if it weren't for the continual pain.

I often thought about how to cope with my frustration and pain. One day I realized that I had been focusing entirely on my body. I needed to do something else.

I hadn't painted for years. I took out my old painting equipment. My folks drove me to the store to buy canvas and new brushes. I spent my spare time painting. I could be engrossed for hours at a time and be unaware of my pain. It was a pleasant distraction and gave me a much needed inner calmness. I painted for nine or ten months. Some of my paintings were shown at the tennis club and at the medical clinic. I had a nice writeup in the clinic newsletter. People called to say they had seen my paintings and that they liked them. Some friends wanted to buy them. I spent much time painting and exercising, but realized that I needed to do more. I needed inner self-healing. I had spent scant time on my spiritual self. With so much pain and medication, concentration was difficult.

After I came home from the hospital, I used visualization to help heal my bedsore. Although some doctors thought that it would never heal without surgery, it healed completely. Then I stopped using visualization.

43

Braces

I had improved so much over the past months, that Diana thought I was ready to be fitted for leg braces. I could hardly wait. I thought that wearing them would enable me to walk.

I was so excited the day that John and I met Diana at the bracemaker's shop. With some help from Diana and John, I held myself up on parallel bars, while the bracemaker wrapped plaster-soaked gauze around my legs, and we waited for the casts to harden.

Finally, the casts were firm enough that I could sit in my wheelchair. He had put rubber tubing under the fronts of the casts, so that when they were hard, he could cut them with a cast saw, without injuring my legs. He said that we could pick up the braces in a few weeks.

When he called to say that the braces were ready, Diana drove me to the shop for the fitting. When he came in with my braces, I was so anxious to try them on that I didn't pay attention to what he was saying. He took off my shoes and put on the braces.

The braces extended from my knees to my feet. They were white plastic with a thick Velcro strap at the top to keep them snug. I was disappointed. Not only were they ugly, but the feet of the braces were covered by an awful pair of men's shoes, size 11. I looked like Minnie Mouse! I didn't want anyone to see me wearing them. But, if they helped me walk, I wouldn't complain.

I spent the next several months trying to walk with the braces. To balance while standing, I needed to bend my knees, but the braces were stiff so that I couldn't bend them. I could barely stand with them on. My anterior thigh muscles were strong, and I could balance better with the braces off than with them on.

With the braces on, my right knee tended to turn inward so that, without warning, my right hip would collapse forward. I couldn't put my weight on that side. I was exasperated. I finally told Diana that the braces weren't right. They had to be shortened so I could bend my knees. She agreed.

"You're not the average paraplegic," said Diana. "I realized that the first week I worked with you. You have an unusual combination of sensory and motor loss. According to the book, you shouldn't have recovered some of the feeling and movement that you have. You surprise me with something new each time I visit."

Diana arranged another visit to the bracemaker. At first, he wasn't willing to alter the braces. He assumed all paraplegics needed locked knee braces. Diana assured him that, as my therapist, she knew it was the right thing to do. She felt that if it weren't for my footdrop, I wouldn't need braces.

He finally agreed to shorten the braces and to remove enough of the lower part of the braces that I could wear my own tennis shoes over them.

After the braces had been remodeled, I tried standing and walking with them for almost a year. The braces still weren't right. One day I was so peeved, I asked John to put them on and see what he thought.

With them on he could hardly prevent himself from

falling backward. With no motion in the ankles, if the braces were swung forward, the toes caught on the floor. It was very difficult to lift them and swing them forward. In addition, the back of the right brace was not perpendicular to the bottom of the brace. That seemed to be the reason my right hip still tended to collapse forward.

John and I decided that going back to the same bracemaker wouldn't achieve anything. There simply were too many things wrong with the braces.

John asked several orthopedic surgeons who else we might try. They suggested someone at Children's Hospital at Stanford, so I made an appointment to have new braces fitted there.

My new bracefitter carefully took my measurements and made casts of my legs and feet. When they were ready, Diana, John, and I were there for the fitting. The braces were in two pieces, front and back, which were strapped together. They were lighter than my first braces. Much to my surprise, they were as confining as my first braces. They were too high. There was no motion in the ankles. When I tried to stand with them on between the parallel bars, I couldn't straighten up. I was so disappointed that I wanted to cry.

Frustrated, I said, "Why is it so difficult for people to listen to what I want?"

Diana told the bracefitter that I wasn't a typical paraplegic. We wanted the braces cut down to the calves and hinges at both ankles.

The bracefitter was reluctant to change them. She had never altered braces that way for a paraplegic. She felt I needed stiff knee and ankle support. After much discussion, she agreed to change them.

After the braces were altered, I was able to stand with

my knees slightly bent. Using my arms for support, I was able to walk. The bracefitter was surprised.

Diana laughed and said, "I told you she was different."

At last I had some functional braces. Supporting myself in part with my arms, I could walk to the end of my parallel bars and back.

Diana brought me a walker. After several attempts, I was able to get up from the wheelchair and stand in the walker. I needed someone to hold the walker firmly until I was standing. Then I had to learn to balance on my feet long enough to lift the walker and move it forward. It took several weeks for me to pull myself up, stand, balance, lift the walker forward, and take a step. Soon I could take several steps.

One day when John came home, I asked him to watch what I could do. With great effort I proudly showed him that I could walk in the walker from the kitchen to my bedroom.

I was doing so well that Diana felt I didn't need her services anymore. In spite of the pain I had come a long way.

44

A Return to Valley

I reached a plateau where I couldn't improve my walking time. There was much stress on my arms and hands. My hands were already painful and arthritic from using the wheelchair.

I talked to John about returning to Valley Medical Center as an outpatient. They had much more equipment than I had at home, and perhaps a therapist there could provide me with some new ideas. I made an appointment, hoping to learn something beneficial.

My folks drove me to Valley Medical Center. After I registered, we went to the gym where I had worked out as an inpatient. My folks waited patiently during the 45 minutes I was tested for muscle strength and flexibility.

When that was finished, the young therapist wanted me to walk between the parallel bars. I wheeled to the bars, pulled myself up, and began to walk. I recalled being there before. Then I had braces to my hips and needed help getting up. When I had finally stood up, I couldn't do much. Now, a year or so later, I could walk the length of the bars four times without stopping. I was elated by my improvement. I couldn't wait to hear what the therapist thought.

He commented, "I think you would balance better if your braces were higher and we got rid of the ankle hinges."

I couldn't believe it. What an idiot! Although I was

irritated, I calmly explained that I balanced better with hinged braces.

"No," he said, "You need more support. All paras need more stability."

I told him I had had longer stiff braces before and had found it difficult to even stand.

"Well," he said, "I know you would do better if you changed them."

I was angry, barely under control. He hadn't learned to listen to patients. He was disregarding what I had told him. He was parroting what he had been taught, as if every paraplegic was the same. I saw no point in talking to him. I let him ramble on. The more he talked, the more he convinced me of his ignorance.

"You will be able to walk again, but you must have your braces altered first. I would like to see you three times a week. I'll set up your appointments while you're here."

I wasn't going to spend $150 an hour to have this novice work with me. I told him to forget it.

I kept thinking there must be someone who could help me to walk. It was depressing to talk to therapists who knew less about what to do for my condition than I did.

45

On My Own

I decided to work harder on my own, and do my exercise routine twice a day instead of once. The increased workout time caused sore muscles and frequent spasms. Some days the spasms were so bad I could barely get out of bed. I thought massages would help.

Before the accident I had worked out regularly at a spa and remembered a masseuse there I had liked. I remembered her face, but couldn't recall her name. I called the spa, but it had changed ownership, and no one there knew who I was talking about.

I called Diana to ask if she could recommend a masseuse. She recommended a place for me to call. When I phoned, I was given the names of two women who made house calls. I was told one of them would call me back. When the call came, I made an appointment for the masseuse to come to my house. That morning I eagerly awaited her arrival. When I answered the door, I was astonished to see the masseuse that had worked on me at the spa. I remembered her name.

"Mary Ann!"

"I remember you! I worked on you before."

We were so excited that we talked non-stop through my massage.

We agreed that I would have a massage once a week.

The treatments relaxed my tight muscles and decreased the number of spasms.

Now, with exercise, acupressure, and massage I thought I had the right program and would improve.

But I pushed too hard. In a few weeks my foot and leg pain were as bad as ever. I also developed back pain. I would have to alter my routine.

Before my accident, when I had pulled something in my back or neck, I occasionally went to a chiropractor. He frequently helped me. I felt it was time to see him again. Since it had been two years since my back surgery, I felt my back was strong enough, that having it adjusted wouldn't be hazardous.

My first appointment with him went well. He took X-rays and talked about what he thought we should do. He asked if I planned to have the rods in my back removed.

"No way. John and I decided no more surgery, unless it's absolutely necessary. I'd have to be in excruciating pain before I'd have more surgery."

He said he understood.

He took measurements to see if my back was aligned and then carefully applied pressure to multiple joints along my spine to make them pop. The treatments decreased my pain. I was confident that massage, acupressure, and manipulation could relieve my pain while I continued to exercise.

46

Thyme

When I went to bed that night, I said my prayers and asked Jesus if there was anything else I could do to heal myself. Because I was afraid of seeing visions, I asked for answers to appear in my dreams.

Before the accident, I had some wonderful dreams. When I was in the hospital, I couldn't remember having a single dream, possibly because of the medication I took. At home I started to dream again, and the dreams were very positive. I never pictured myself in a wheelchair. I saw myself limping or trying to help an infant walk. In about a half dozen dreams I was playing tennis. In them I asked for a long warmup so I'd be ready to play. Each time I told the other players to be patient with me, since it had been a long time since I'd played. I accepted that I wasn't as good a player as I had been. I was pleased just to be on the court having fun.

That night I dreamed I was baking a loaf of special herbal bread. I placed the uncooked bread in the oven and watched it through the glass door of the oven. I could see it turning golden-brown. I went to the counter to check the recipe. I realized that I had left out the most important ingredient, a special herb. I quickly turned around and asked those nearby if anyone had the special herb that should be added to the bread. Someone extended a small jar toward me. As I reached for the jar, it fell to the floor, and many little brown herbs spilled out. They looked like the cloves that are put on ham.

"What kind of herb is that?" I asked.

A voice replied, "It's THYME!"

I understood the message. Sometimes I pushed too hard. I realized I couldn't hurry TIME, no matter how hard I tried. I would walk when the time was right and not before.

47

A Spirit Guide

For a week the pain had been unrelenting. I thought I would go crazy. I frequently cried and sometimes screamed. Before the accident I could relieve stress by aerobics or dancing. Now all I could do was scream as loud as I could and cry till there were no more tears. That night, in my prayers, I told the Lord I would give up any hope of walking if He would just take away the pain.

When I finished my prayers, I rolled over on my stomach to try to sleep. As I was almost asleep, I heard the sound of a footstep on a loose floorboard in the hall. As I listened, I felt the bed move as if someone had sat on the edge of the bed. I lifted my head to see if John was there. I saw no one. I was frightened and could feel my heart pounding. I was sure there was a spirit in my room. I remembered from one of my classes that if you ask a spirit guide to leave, it would.

"If anyone is in this room, please leave," I asked.

"God is with me. No harm can come to me," I said over and over.

When I stopped, the house was quiet. I turned the light on. It was over an hour before I could fall asleep. I left the light on all night.

The next day Julie came to give me acupressure. I told her what had happened the night before and how scared I was.

"Honestly, Bev, you're always so frightened over these things. Nothing bad is going to happen to you. You're a good person. I think if it happens again, you should let it come through."

I thought, "It's hard to be brave in the middle of the night with the lights out, especially when you feel something sitting on the bed and you don't see anyone."

We talked about it for awhile. I felt better. Maybe she was right. I promised her that if it happened again, I would be brave and welcome the spirit into my room. I really didn't think it would happen again, so I wasn't worried about keeping my promise.

That night, after I went to bed, I thought about the night before and was reluctant to turn off the light. Perhaps there hadn't been a spirit there. Maybe I had dreamed it all. Finally, I convinced myself that it wouldn't happen again. I was no longer afraid. I rolled over on my stomach and turned out the light. I said my prayers and tried to sleep.

I was aware how quiet the house was. Then I heard the same footfall in the hallway. Breathing as quietly as I could, I waited. Again the bed moved as if someone were sitting on it. I remembered my promise to Julie.

I quietly said, "If you are my spirit healer, I welcome you."

Instantly, I felt a whirling mass of energy circling over my lower back. I tried to lift my head, but I couldn't. As the energy spun around, it became stronger. I was sinking into the mattress, and my body felt heavy. I couldn't move. Then the force lessened and was gone. I lay there, afraid to move.

As I thought about what had happened, I was sure I had had a healing! I wondered if I was well enough to stand and walk. I thought about trying then, but I was exhausted and decided to wait until morning. I fell asleep.

The next morning when I awoke, I thought I would be

able to walk. I believed I had experienced a miracle. I sat up and pulled my legs over the side of the bed.

"Well, here goes," I thought.

I repeatedly tried to stand but couldn't. I finally realized that I wasn't as completely healed as I had hoped. I was disappointed. I had expected a miraculous return to normal, but it hadn't happened. Still, I was excited about the experience and thought I had had a healing. I told John what had happened and asked what he thought of it.

"It doesn't surprise me," he said. "You've had many amazing experiences."

The next night I again heard the sound in the hall and felt someone sitting on the bed. I welcomed my spirit healer. Immediately, I felt the energy force on my lower back. This time it wasn't as strong, and soon it was gone. I didn't know what to think. From such a beautiful and exciting experience I had expected more improvement. I hadn't seen a dramatic change, but perhaps I had improved more than I knew.

The night of February 11th I dreamed a woman came to my home. She was expecting other people to come to my home shortly. During the dream, something pushed so hard on my lower back that I woke up. I turned to see who was there, but I couldn't see anything. I turned on the light. No one was there.

The next evening I again awakened from a dream as something pushed on my lower back. The sensations seemed so real. Each time the pressure on my back awakened me and didn't disappear until I turned to see who was there. I never saw anything.

48

Visualization

As I thought about these experiences, I wondered if visualization would enhance my healing. I had learned the technique while studying hypnosis. At that time I realized that I had used visualization since I was a child. I hadn't realized that it was something special. In high school when I entertained, I liked to dance and pantomime to records of Al Jolson, Jerry Lewis, and others. Whenever I practiced, I saw the character in my mind. I never looked in the mirror. I lost my identity and became the performer I was pantomiming. It seemed to work well. Many people enjoyed my performances and commented that I even looked like the people I pantomimed.

I also used visualization during self-hypnosis and for my tennis and art work.

To use visualization to heal my back, I needed to see pictures of the parts of my back: the bones, muscles, and nerves. I studied my back X-rays. John showed me diagrams of the back in his anatomy book. He showed me where my back had been broken and where the rods were placed. I concentrated on the pictures and tried to absorb all the information.

Then I went to my room to meditate and think about the healing. I began the visualization by calling Jesus and seeing him standing over me. I visualized Him placing his hands on the top of my head. From Him a beautiful lavender light slowly filled the inside of my body. As I saw the light flowing, I felt its warmth. I could see inside my body, the bones, muscles, nerves, and the rods in my back. I could see and feel the light entering my head and gently flowing through the shoulders, arms, and chest. When it reached my back, it slowed and surrounded my spine. Its warmth healed. As the light reached my leg muscles, I saw them come alive. I watched delicate white nerves regenerating. As the light of Christ touched my injuries, I knew they were healing. Using my mind and the spirit within me, I felt balanced and at peace.

Rod Surgery

49

Getting Worse

April 27th would be the second anniversary of the day of my accident, the day I had barely been given the chance to continue living. I imagine most people expected me to be depressed that day, thinking of the horrible accident and how it changed my life. But I had survived. I had been given a second chance, when two of my friends had not.

I decided to celebrate April 27th as my survival day. A few friends were bringing me lunch that day, not realizing what that day meant to me. I bought napkins, paper plates, a few small noisemakers, and a cake.

When my friends walked into the family room, they were surprised to see the cake.

"Hey, wait a minute," said Judy. "Your birthday is in October."

"You're right," I replied. "This is my survival day, the day I was reborn. I'm not the same Beverly I was two years ago. My life has changed greatly, and I believe it's made me a better human being. So it's a day to celebrate."

"That's great," said Betty.

"I never thought of it that way," Marilyn said, "but you're right. We should celebrate."

During the previous two years, I'd worked hard. I remembered when I couldn't move from the waist down and had almost no sensation in my legs or posterior thighs. Now I had some feeling in my right leg down to the ankle.

In my left leg I had feeling to just below the knee. I could move my thighs easily and walk a little bit with the help of a walker. I was convinced that I would be walking on my own in another year, especially if my pain went away.

By May I experienced more pain than I had had in two years. I couldn't understand it. Since the doctors had assured me that my pain was from nerve regeneration, I felt I wasn't damaging anything by continuing my therapy, so I pushed as hard as I could. I could feel and see that the muscles in my thighs and legs were getting stronger. Although this encouraged me, I soon couldn't sit up for an hour. I spent most of the day lying down, and a good part of it crying.

In addition to the leg and foot pain that I always had, I now had pain in my lower back and around the tailbone. Whenever I tried to sit, I felt tremendous pressure around the tailbone. I thought there must be something wrong with the rods for me to have so much pain.

John took me to see several doctors. Although they weren't sure why my pain was increasing, they thought it might be phantom pain. I told them that I could feel the rods, and I thought they were moving. I was told I couldn't possibly feel them. They were anchored to the vertebrae so they couldn't move.

Time passed very slowly.

I told John, "Something is very wrong with my back. I'm sure it's the rods. I don't care what the doctors say. I know my body better than they do. I know what I feel."

"Okay, Babe. I think it's time to get some X-rays of your back. If you think it's the rods, we better check it out. Anyway, it's been a year since your last X-rays. They should be repeated."

208

Friday, June 2nd I went to the clinic for X-rays. The films showed that my rods had moved a centimeter. John and I had decided earlier that I wouldn't have the rods removed unless they were causing me unbearable pain. The pain was fierce, but I didn't want to go through another surgery. John knew how upset I was and how much pain I had. He told me he would talk to several doctors, so we could decide what should be done.

50

Agonizing Pain

The next morning John had gone to work. I was home alone and in my wheelchair. As I bent down and twisted to the left, I felt something move in my back, accompanied by a sharp, stabbing pain. I knew it was the rods. In severe pain I wheeled to bed and lay down. I knew something dreadful had happened.

I called John at work and told him what had happened. He came home immediately. The pain was unbearable. I was crying uncontrollably.

John called the clinic and found that my doctor was not in and not on call. He asked the operator to have whoever was on call in orthopedics call him at home right away. He gave the operator his name and number, and the operator told him the doctor would call him back. It seemed like forever before the doctor called. John explained what had happened. The doctor gave him the names and numbers of two physicians who specialized in Harrington rods. When John called those numbers he reached answering services. Although both surgeons were off for the weekend and one was not expected in till Tuesday, John asked the operators to have the physicians call him when they checked in with the answering service.

John gave me as many pain pills as he thought was safe. They made me groggy but only dulled the pain a little.

The phone rang. One of the surgeons had returned

John's call and said he would be in his office Tuesday. He told John to call on Monday to make an appointment for me. John was very upset about the delay and tried to think of someone else he might call. He finally calmed down and thought about what I would need to survive the weekend.

"With the amount of pain you're having, you're going to need more pain medication than we have here."

John can't write prescriptions for narcotics. He phoned a physician friend of his and explained the situation. His friend agreed to write a prescription for me and to meet John at the clinic, so John could pick up the prescription and have it filled.

"I'll have to leave you for about an hour to pick up the prescription. Do you think you'll be all right?"

"I'll manage," I said.

John left.

I was in great pain, alone, and frightened. I decided to call Diana. When I heard her voice, I began to sob, and it was difficult for her to understand me. She questioned me, and I had trouble answering.

She said she would come over right away, and until she arrived, to keep talking on the phone to her roommate Debbie, who was also a friend of mine. Debbie asked me to keep talking to her. My speech was slurred, and I didn't want to talk anymore.

I was thinking, "Why is she making me talk? I'm tired and feel like I want to die."

"I don't want to talk anymore," I cried. "I don't want to live like this. I can't take any more pain."

"I know, Bev. It's not fair. Diana will be there soon. We will get you some help as soon as we can."

I was still on the phone when Diana arrived. I was so

211

happy to see her. She took the phone from me and told Debbie to come over.

Both John and Debbie arrived. I was glad Diana and Debbie were there. John needed support. He was tired and stressed.

Debbie worked at Stanford Children's Hospital with the other surgeon that John had tried to call. Debbie knew where to locate him and phoned him immediately. She explained the situation and asked if he would help. He told her that he usually worked with children and seldom with adults.

Debbie was persuasive. He finally agreed to see me Monday morning at Stanford Children's Hospital.

"Oh, my God," I cried when she told me the news. "How am I going to last till Monday? This is only Saturday. I don't think I can last that long with this horrible pain."

"You're going to have to, Babe," John said. "We don't have a choice."

"Can you sit up, Bev?" Diana asked.

"No, I can't even turn from side to side. John has to carefully roll me from one side to the other. I feel as if I have a knife stuck in my back. Every time I move, I can feel the rods."

"She's not going to be able to sit in a car," Diana told John. "It might be wise to get an ambulance. If you like, I will take care of it for you."

John agreed. He was thankful for the help.

After Diana and Debbie were sure we were all right, they left.

John had to take care of me and our two thirteen year old dogs. John had just taken Troy, our Great Dane mix, to a vet to have a gum tumor removed. Since the surgery Troy had been sick and had not eaten. John hand fed him and put water in his mouth for him to drink. Nike, our husky-shepherd, had kidney disease and spent much of her time drinking and going outside to tinkle. Day and night John checked on me, gave me pain medication, and turned me.

51

To the Hospital

Finally, Monday morning at 8:30 the ambulance arrived. Two men with a stretcher came in and gently rolled me on to it. With some difficulty they were able to get me around the corner in the hall, place me on a gurney, and get me into the ambulance parked on our steep driveway. Every movement hurt me. John said he would follow the ambulance to Stanford Children's Hospital.

When the ambulance doors slammed shut, it brought back memories. A few weeks earlier when John and I were in our car, we heard a siren and saw the blinking red lights of an ambulance. I had turned to John and said, "Boy, I hope I never need another ride in one of those. I remember how painful the rides were."

"I hope you don't have to either, Babe. I think you've had your share."

Well, again I was in another damned ambulance. Every time its speed increased, the bumps jolted me more and the pain was worse. I couldn't believe this was happening to me again.

"Dear Jesus," I thought, "when are you going to let up on me? I can't take much more."

I began to cry. I was surprised that I had tears left.

Finally we arrived at the hospital. The ambulance doors opened. The attendants wheeled me into the hospital. Diana was waiting outside for me and Debby inside. John

214

had followed the ambulance. I was glad they were there.

I was taken downstairs to a reception desk with a pleasant lady behind it. She told us that they were usually closed Monday morning and the surgeon was coming in just to see me. I had arrived a little early and had to wait on a gurney in the hall until the doctor arrived.

The ambulance attendants waited until I was moved into a treatment room so they could have their gurney back. They wanted to know if they should wait to transfer me from Stanford Children's Hospital to Stanford Medical Center.

The gurney was uncomfortable. Although John had given me pain pills before we left the house, the pain was still severe.

When the surgeon arrived, John told him my complex medical history. John had brought all my back X-rays, including those done three days ago. The surgeon examined them and agreed that the rods had moved. However, he felt that I had too much pain to attribute it all to rod movement. He thought the pain was caused by something more serious. Since my most painful episode had occurred after the last films were taken, he wanted to take more to see if the rods had moved closer to the spinal canal.

John took my X-rays to one of the hospital radiologists to have him look for anything else that might be causing my pain. John returned to say that the only thing apparently wrong was the movement of the rods.

I was wheeled into a radiology room for more films. Hearing that no one knew what was causing my pain made me tense. When I'm tense, I have more pain. I felt my pain was due to the rods and was disappointed to hear that the surgeon doubted it. I tried to stay calm and repeatedly said to myself, "Relax." I cried in pain when I was moved onto the small X-ray table.

Being on my back for the first film wasn't too bad because they didn't move me much. But for the second film they wanted me on my side with my knees close to my chest. When they tried to bring my knees up, I screamed with pain. The rods stabbed me, and the pain was excruciating. I became hysterical. I wanted to die. Although they couldn't place me in an ideal position, they took more X-rays. After the films were developed, they gently turned me on my back. The pain eased some.

John tried to calm me. I squeezed his hand hard.

"It's all right, Babe," he said. "They have all the films they need. They're reviewing the new ones to see if they can tell if the rods are causing the pain. The surgeon has never seen rods give anyone this much pain."

"I know it's the rods. I can feel them. How can he say it isn't? I know what I feel. Why doesn't anyone listen to me?" I cried.

"Calm down, Babe, I believe you. We'll get them removed."

"If the doctor had these rods in his back, he would believe me."

As the surgeon showed John the X-rays, he pointed out that the larger rod had moved 1.5 cm and one hook had come off the rod. The smaller rod was bent. Everyone was surprised that I could have bent one of the metal rods.

The doctor told John that the rods needed to be removed. I could have told him that without X-rays.

The surgeon asked John if he wanted a neurosurgeon to assist in the surgery. John said yes and chose a neurosurgeon that he had known for a long time. The surgeon left the room to call the neurosurgeon to arrange a time that both of them would be available for surgery.

Diana and Debbie stayed by me when they could. We all hoped that I could be admitted to Stanford Medical Center that day. I never thought I would look forward to surgery, but I couldn't tolerate more pain. I felt tremendous pressure on my tailbone. Pain was going down my legs and feet. I could feel the rods sticking in my lower back.

"Please let there be someone who can help me," I prayed.

The surgeon returned and informed us that the only day the two surgeons could get together was Friday.

"Oh my God!" I yelled. "Today is only Monday. That means four more days of pain. Oh, John, I can't handle it. I know I'll die before Friday from the pain."

John held my hand with both of his. He asked if the surgery couldn't be done sooner. The surgeon told John that I could have surgery as an emergency patient, but he didn't recommend it. I would have to take my chances with the surgeons and anesthesiologist on call that day. The surgeon would probably know little about Harrington rods.

John said, "Babe, I want the best surgeons to work on you. I know it's going to be tough, but I think we should wait. I don't think we should try to keep you in the hospital until Friday. I doubt we can get a bed. I honestly think I can take better care of you at home than the interns and residents will in the hospital. I can be at your side in seconds, and I know you won't get that kind of attention in the hospital. At home you will have privacy. I can give you pain medication when you need it. You can sleep whenever you can, and I will see that you aren't disturbed."

I knew he was right. I just hoped I could handle it. John

would arrange for me to be brought by ambulance to Stanford Medical Center at 8 AM on Friday, June 9th. The other arrangements would be made by the doctors and their staff. My back surgery was scheduled for that day.

I was disappointed and exhausted. I wasn't looking forward to the ride home or waiting four days for surgery.

The ambulance arrived, and I was again placed on a gurney and put in the ambulance. I hated being there. The gurney was hard, and the constant motion was painful. I tried to think of something pleasant, but the pain was too great and I couldn't concentrate.

Finally, we arrived home. John had followed us. I was glad to be home so I could get out of the ambulance. The attendants carried me into my bedroom and gently placed me on my bed. They tried to make me comfortable and then left.

52

Home Awaiting Surgery

"Oh, John, I don't know if I can last four days. The pain is awful. All I want to do is cry and scream."

"Hon, I know it's awful, but everything will eventually be all right. I'll be with you all the time to get what you need and turn you to a more comfortable position. I'll keep notes to be sure you get your medications on time, and I have enough meds to last until Friday. I have someone to cover for me at work. We have enough food in the house."

"John, can a person die from too much pain?"

"Pain can stress your heart or cause you to faint. That's not going to happen to you. You're very strong or you wouldn't have come this far."

"I don't feel strong now." I began to cry. "It's not fair, John. For two years I've tried so hard to get better. I'm worse now than when I came home from Valley Medical Center."

"No, honey, you're not worse. You've forgotten how bad you were. I feel strongly that the rods are causing your pain. When they're out, you'll see a big difference."

"Maybe you're right. This could be a blessing in disguise. But why do I have to suffer so much?"

"Remember we had decided not to have the rods removed unless it was absolutely necessary? You had said, 'No more surgery.' If the pain hadn't been this severe, we might not have agreed to have the rods removed. I believe

219

you will be much better off with the rods out."

"Well, somebody up there has gotten my attention. I just wish He would ease my pain."

The next four days were the longest and most difficult in my life. It was just as hard on John. He was tired. He frequently rolled me from side to side so I wouldn't develop a bedsore. What bothered him most was that I was in constant pain. The pain pills and muscle relaxants helped some, but I was never free from pain. One night the pain was so great, that I began to cry uncontrollably. John lay down beside me and held me in his arms. He had tears in his eyes.

My folks came by every day and brought us dinner. It was hard for them to see me like this. Their eyes often filled with tears as they saw my pain. I felt badly that I was causing so much stress to my family. It was frustrating not to be able to do anything. I worried about the muscles I had worked so hard on the last two years. How much would I lose by lying flat in bed for a week and then for sometime after surgery? God knows how long I'd be in bed after the operation.

John tried to reassure me that I would be better once the rods were out and that I wouldn't lose that much. I didn't think about anything when the pain was severe, but when the pain eased up, I worried about everything.

53

Surgery

I was so happy when Friday morning came. I was looking forward to being rid of the pain. The ambulance arrived and transported me to Stanford Medical Center. John followed the ambulance.

I had been assigned to a two-bed room in the neurosurgical ward on the second floor, and John accompanied me there. The ambulance attendants transferred me to my bed, wished me well, and left. When John saw that I was settled, he returned to the admissions desk to fill out the necessary forms.

I had blood drawn for tests prior to surgery.

The surgery was scheduled for 2:30 PM. I remembered that surgery at Stanford Medical Center often started later than it was scheduled. My kidney surgery had been six hours late.

I told John, "I hope the surgery will be on time. I hate waiting. I've waited long enough."

"I agree," said John. "You've suffered enough."

Much to our surprise, the nurse came in to tell us that I would be going to pre-op about 1:00 PM. Sure enough, a little before 1:00, two surgery attendants came and transferred me to a gurney. John followed as they wheeled me to the pre-op room. When we arrived, John asked the nurse there if he could wait with me until I went into surgery. She said he could, if he would put on a cap, gown, and shoe covers. John put on the garments the nurse had requested. He looked like a comedian in a hospital movie. I couldn't help laughing.

I had been taken into the new surgical wing at Stanford Medical Center. John was impressed with the new facilities, and the nurses told him how happy they were there. He stood by my gurney and held my hand, reassuring me that everything would be fine. The anesthesiologist came out to talk to me. John was elated to see that it was a friend of his, and he introduced him to me. After the anesthesiologist asked me a few questions and told me what the anesthetic would be like, he said that I would soon be going into the operating room. Then he left.

John said, "We're really fortunate. You have an excellent orthopedic surgeon, neurosurgeon, and anesthesiologist. I'm sure everything is going to go well."

In a few minutes they came to take me into the operating room.

I looked at John and whispered, "I love you."

He smiled and said, "I love you, too. I'll be waiting for you when you come out."

I knew he would be. He was always there for me. How I loved him!

They wheeled me into the operating room. The anesthesiologist said he was going to give me an injection. I was to start counting backward, starting with 99. The last thing I remember was saying 98.

54

Recovery

The next I knew, I awoke in the recovery room. I couldn't believe the surgery was over. I didn't feel sick. I didn't have any pain. I remembered talking to the nurses in the room, but couldn't remember what I said.

After I had been in the recovery room for a while, I was ready to return to the ward. As they wheeled me into the hall, I saw John coming toward me. He looked worried and tired.

"Hi, Babe," he said. " How are you feeling?"

"I'm feeling fine. I'm glad it's over."

"I can't believe how alert you are and in such good spirits. It's amazing."

Soon after I was back in bed, I fell asleep. When I awoke, I was lying on my back. I didn't think I should be lying on my incision, but it didn't feel sore. I turned my head and saw John. I don't know how long he had been waiting for me to wake up, but I was happy to see his face.

He told me the surgeons said the surgery had been successful. We were happy with how smoothly everything had gone.

"How are the dogs doing?" I asked.

"Troy isn't doing well. I'm worried about him."

"Why don't you go home and spend some time with him?"

"Do you think you are going to be all right?"

"Yes, I'll probably sleep through the night."

He leaned over and kissed me.

"I'll call you tonight and see you tomorrow," he said.

The next day I was still feeling good. My IV was hooked up to a machine that would release pain medication into my vein when I pressed a button. It would release a certain amount and then couldn't be used again for 15 minutes. There was a clock attached to it so I could tell when I could have another dose. I couldn't give myself an overdose. I used it frequently that day.

With my pain under control, I decided to try sitting up. I raised the head of my bed to a sitting position.

"Not bad," I thought.

John was amazed that I could sit up without difficulty. I was so happy that, with the rods removed, the stabbing pain was gone. With medication, the pain from the surgery was not too bad.

My folks came. They were relieved to see how well I felt.

The orthopedic surgeon came by. He was pleased to see me sitting up. He told me that he had never seen rods as loose as mine.

"You made a believer of me. The larger rod was so loose that I was able to lift it out easily. The hook at the bottom of the large rod had slipped off. I understand now why you had so much pain. The thinner steel rod was slightly bent. I cut it in two to remove it. You must have been very active."

"Well, I did a lot of physical therapy," I said with a smile.

"Your back looked good. We didn't have to do a bone graft or replace the rods. The third and fourth vertebrae, the ones that were fused previously, have healed nicely. You have a strong and healthy back. I'm sure you'll find that you have more freedom of movement. That should make you happy."

224

"Thanks, doc. It sounds like you did a great job."

"Don't thank me. I only removed the rods and sewed you up. You do the healing."

I had very little pain. It was almost as if I hadn't had back surgery. I hadn't realized how much the rods had restricted my back movement. Without the rods I could turn, twist, and bend forward and to the sides.

That night Stephanie came to visit. I was so happy to see her. Although she was seven months pregnant, she had driven alone from Davis to see me. I appreciated her visit.

When Sunday came, I was still feeling pretty good. I didn't like taking pain medication, so I decided to take less. Without the medication, the pain soon returned. I felt a sharp pain in the top of my hand where the IV was placed. I saw that the entire top of my hand was swollen. I rang for the nurse. When she came, she saw that the IV fluid was leaking under my skin.

"I'll have to move the IV to another vein."

"Oh, no," I thought, "not again."

Starting an IV in my veins was never easy. I dreaded having someone do it again. After the nurse removed the needle, I could see my hand was swollen and badly bruised. She was looking for another vein.

"I think you'll have a hard time finding another one," I said.

"I'm pretty good at this. We'll find a vein, I'm sure."

I'd heard that before. It seemed that all the medical personnel think they're experts at sticking veins. The majority aren't.

"Oh, well," I thought. "I'll let her take a stab at it."

She tied a piece of rubber tubing around my upper arm and told me to make a fist. She poked and slapped my arm to make the veins stand out.

"Ah," she said, "there's a good one."

I closed my eyes. Watching a needle going into me always made me dizzy. At least an arm stick doesn't hurt as much as one in the back of the hand. I clenched my teeth as I felt the needle.

"Darn," she said, "I missed."

My eyes filled with tears. It wasn't so much the pain, as thinking about how many times I would have to be stuck before she was successful. She could tell I was upset.

"I'm going to send for an expert to do this," she said. "Your veins are difficult to stick. They tend to collapse once the needle is inserted."

I was relieved that she didn't persist.

When the expert arrived she said, "I hear you have difficult veins. Let's see what I can do."

She picked a vein in the back of my hand, a site I disliked because it's so painful. To my surprise, she hit the vein on the first try. Was I relieved to have that over!

I was exhausted. Although my back pain was severe, I was determined not to take more pain medication. I thought I could handle it.

When a nurse checked the machine to see how much medication I had taken, she was not pleased to find that I had taken very little. She could tell I hurt.

"How do you expect to heal when you're having pain? Your body needs to be relaxed, not tense. With all the stress, it will take you longer to heal. Now start taking the medication again."

"All right," I said. "I just don't want to get hooked on this stuff."

"Don't worry. We watch out for that."

I pushed the button for more medication, and soon I felt much better.

My son Ken called from Arizona. I was glad to hear his voice. He wanted to fly home to see me, but I told him to wait until I was home.

My folks came whenever they could. I appreciated having such a caring family.

John arrived later in the day. I could tell by the look on his face that something was wrong.

"Hon, what's the matter?" I asked.

His eyes filled with tears.

"I had to put Troy to sleep this morning. He hasn't been eating or drinking, and last night he started passing blood. I knew the anesthetic had badly damaged him, but I kept hoping he would improve. He was too old to have surgery. I couldn't let him suffer any more."

"Oh, John," I cried. "What else can happen to us?"

I felt badly that Troy was gone, but I knew it was harder on John. Troy was John's favorite and followed him everywhere.

With all the stress of the last two weeks, I wondered how John would survive. I had to get better quickly, so I could give him some support.

"I know God will give us a break now. He knows we've suffered enough," I said as I held John's hand.

I wanted to be home with John. He needed me there. At least Nike would be there to greet him and keep him company. I worried about him. It was frustrating.

I thought, "What good am I to anyone? I can't help my own husband when he needs me. Everybody has to help me. I hate it!"

By ten that night I was so frustrated and angry that I was

having muscle spasms in my thighs and legs. When the nurse came, she found an unhappy, frustrated, angry, sobbing woman in severe pain. I told her what had happened and how I felt. She told me to press the button for pain medicine. She brought me a muscle relaxant and a sleeping pill.

"Now," she said, "that should be enough for you to have a good night's sleep. Things will look better in the morning."

"Sure," I thought. "I've heard that before. That's what Mom said to me when I was growing up."

Maybe there's some truth to that saying. The next morning I felt better. My IV was removed.

My roommate Sally had heard us talking about Troy the day before. She told me she was sorry. We talked through breakfast. I felt like we were old friends. I was lucky to have a good roommate.

Sally had been upset. She had come from Los Angeles for neck surgery, and it had been cancelled because she had a cold. She was feeling better now. Her surgery was scheduled for Wednesday morning. She walked in the halls several times a day. How I wished I could have done that. I needed some way to work off frustration. I could only cry.

When Sally left for her morning walk, I had a chance to do some thinking. I decided that today, my third day in the hospital, was the day I would discontinue my pain medication. I wanted to get in a wheelchair. I felt I was ready to go home.

When John arrived, I told him of my plans.

"I'm not sure you're ready to go home yet," he said.

"I'm fine," I assured him. "Get the nurse and tell her I need a wheelchair."

The nurse said there wasn't a wheelchair on the ward,

but that John might be able to borrow one at the admissions desk. In about twenty minutes John came in with a wheelchair. The nurse wanted him to help her lift me into the chair.

"I don't need to be lifted," I said indignantly. "I can do it on my own."

"Not while I'm on duty," she said.

"If you must help, how about just holding on to me. I know I can transfer to the chair without any help."

"Well, all right."

She held onto me tightly, as if she thought I was going to fall. I didn't realize how weak I was from lying in bed for ten days. I barely was able to transfer to the chair. I was glad she held on, but I didn't tell her.

I was happy to be up and around with so little back pain. I felt like a new person. Things were going to be better. John wheeled me through the halls of the hospital. We were happy that I was doing so well.

"We're on our way," I said. "Do you think I can go home today?"

"We'll have to ask the doctor. You know, Babe, it's only been three days since your surgery. You have an eight-inch incision in your back. It's going to take time to heal."

"I don't even feel it. I have no pain!"

"That's great, but I don't think you should rush things. I don't want you to be disappointed if you can't go home right away."

John didn't know I'd already focused on going home that day or the next.

"Don't worry. I'm a lot better than you think."

John wheeled me back to the room and helped me into bed. I really wanted to go home. I knew he would feel better if I were there.

It was about 11:00 AM when we returned to the room.

While we were talking, a nurse came in and asked how my ride had been.

"Terrific," I replied. "I'm ready to go home today."

"You can't go home today. You just had surgery," said the nurse.

"There's no need for me to stay here. I'm really doing well. I don't need any more pain medicine. I can wheel around just fine."

"Has the doctor changed the dressing on your back yet?"

"No, not yet," I replied.

"Well, that's something that must be done. Also, before you can leave, the doctor must sign your release papers and leave them at the nurse's station."

"Okay. What time will the doctor be in today?"

"He's usually here by 10:00, but I haven't seen him this morning."

"Good, I have a chance to catch him this morning."

"Mrs. Differding, I don't think it's wise for you to go home so soon. I'm sure the doctor will feel the same way. Please don't get your hopes too high."

"We'll see," I replied.

Around 11:45 that morning, the orthopedic surgeon came in with the nurse. I was happy to see him.

"You're just the man I wanted to see."

"Well, you're just the patient I wanted to see," he said jokingly. "I need to look at your back and change the dressing."

I leaned forward so that he could remove my bandage and check the incision. Then he applied a clean dressing.

"You're healing nicely. Everything looks good. When you get home, you can start exercising. Your back is strong and you don't have to worry about injuring it."

"Aha," I thought. "This is the perfect time to ask."

"Since I'm doing so well, do you think I can go home?"

"I don't see why not," he said.

"Can you sign me out today?"

"I'd be glad to, but I can't. You're on the neurosurgeon's floor. He has to sign you out."

"Well, thanks anyway," I said. "I thought I'd give it a try."

The doctor left. I was disappointed, but I wasn't going to give up.

As the nurse left, she remarked, "I still think it's too soon for you to be going home."

John said, "I think the nurse might be right, Babe. Maybe you shouldn't rush it."

I didn't respond. He gave me a kiss and left.

Soon after John left, the neurosurgeon came by. He said I would be ready to go home the next day. Hurray! Tomorrow would be soon enough. I couldn't wait to tell John. I knew I could do it. I was so happy that I would be leaving.

I couldn't wait to tell my nurse.

"I don't believe it," she said.

Another nurse said, "I've never seen anyone that had back surgery go home so soon. You are a very strong lady."

I hadn't thought about being strong, but it seemed I was, both physically and mentally. When I wanted something badly enough, I focused on it in my mind, until I actually saw it happening. I'd been amazed at some of the things I'd accomplished since my accident. **The challenges of the last two years have made me aware of it.**

That evening I told John the good news.

231

55

Going Home

Nine o'clock Tuesday morning, I was ready to go home. John came with my wheelchair. As I said good-bye to my roommate Sally, we hugged with tears in our eyes. We promised to keep in touch. I transferred to my chair, and John wheeled me to the nurse's station. They checked to be sure that everything was in order for my release. The nurses said they hated to see me leave, because I was such a good patient. They each gave me a hug and said good-bye.

John wheeled me down the hall to the elevator. Then we were on the main floor and finally outside. I was so glad to be able to sit in our car. I hated ambulance rides. I prayed that I'd need one again. John and I were happy that I was going home. I felt good!

As we drove home, I realized that if I hadn't suffered so much, I would never have had the surgery. If I hadn't had the surgery, I would never have known how well my back had healed or known the freedom of movement I had without the rods. I hadn't needed a fusion or more rods put in. I remembered the spirit healings I had experienced a few months ago. The spirit had healed my back! That's probably why my surgery and recovery had gone so well.

When I returned home, Nike greeted me. She wasn't able to jump up and put her feet in my lap. I gave her a big hug and scratched her behind her ears. She wasn't her usual happy self, though her tail slowly wagged.

"John, what's wrong with Nike?"

"She's sick and I think she misses Troy. She's been sad since he's been gone. She used to stay with Troy, but now she follows me."

Dogs react to losing their mates, just like humans do. I felt sorry for her and hoped she would improve. She hardly ate and seldom left her bed except to go outside.

Ken came home from Arizona to see how I was doing. John was happy that he was home because Ken was Nike's favorite. John noticed that Nike was starting to cough and had fluid in her lungs. We realized that it was time to say good-bye to Nike. We all petted her, telling her what a good dog she was. John took her to the vet to put her to sleep. When he returned without her, I knew she was gone.

"When Nike walked up to the vet's door," John said, "she scratched to get in. She had always been afraid to go to the vet. It was as if she was anxious to go. The vet examined her and said that her heart was enlarged and her lungs were full of fluid. She was clearly suffering. The vet agreed that she should be put to sleep. I held her head while she was given an injection. She died peacefully. I should have been aware sooner that she was suffering. I just didn't want to lose either dog."

We had tears in our eyes. It took us awhile to get over the shock. It was hard to believe that we had lost both dogs within a week.

When Troy died, John and I agreed to get another dog. John wanted another Great Dane. Since I couldn't control a pup, we wanted a trained dog about a year old.

One of John's friends had seen a newspaper ad for an eight-month-old female Great Dane. John drove to Sunny-vale to see her. She was from a litter of two black females, and her sister had already been sold. The owner was anxious to get rid of her. She had been kept outside in a cage and wasn't allowed in the house. She snarled at John when he entered her cage but had not tried to bite him. She was thin, because the owner had limited her food to keep her from growing too large. Her shoulders slouched when she walked, because she had not had enough exercise.

John drove me to see her. I thought, with love, she would be fine. I wrote a check to the owner, and the owner gave us a leash and some dog food. John put her in the back seat and we took her home.

We decided to call her Mandy. She weighed 90 pounds. John took her to our vet, who noted that she had a good coat, but needed more food and exercise.

We had been spoiled by our old dogs who were calm and loving. Mandy was the opposite. She was hyperactive and curious. She sniffed everything and chewed on many things she found. She was fearful of other people and growled at them and at other dogs. She dug holes in the backyard and pulled branches off bushes.

It was clear she needed obedience training.

She hadn't replaced our old dogs; she had only made us miss them.

I was doing all right. Although I no longer had back pain, my leg and foot pain returned. It bothered me mostly at night, making it difficult to sleep. I decided to take a sleeping pill at night instead of a pain pill, so I wouldn't become addicted.

56

Memory Loss

Months later I noticed I was forgetting things and had a hard time concentrating. When I complained to John, he didn't take me seriously. He found excuses for me, such as there is some loss in old age, that I was overly stressed, that the pain distracted me, that I worried about too many things, and so on.

It was getting worse and I was really worried. I would forget what I was saying in the middle of a sentence. I had trouble understanding what I was reading or would forget what I had read. When I was playing bridge, I couldn't remember what the bid was or what had been played.

One day when I was playing the hand, I couldn't remember what trump was. I had never had problems like that before. I was so embarrassed that when my friends were ready to leave, I apologized for my play and promised to do better the next time.

When they were gone I went to my bedroom to lie down. I settled down with my portable phone close at hand. I was depressed, so I decided to call Mom. I couldn't understand why I wasn't getting a dial tone on my push button phone. I tried to push the buttons anyway. I couldn't find the right numbers and began to get angry. Then I realized that I was trying to dial on the remote control for the TV. I knew something was terribly wrong.

That night I told John what had happened. Since I had

been unconscious after my accident and had not been able to see well when I awoke, I imagined that my current problems were due to brain damage. I was frightened and began to cry. John tried to comfort me. We went to bed early and watched TV.

As I was switching channels, I heard the word Halcion mentioned. I paid attention because that was the sleeping pill I was taking. The program mentioned that it had recently been found to cause forgetfulness, confusion, and, in some cases, violent behavior. We were astounded.

"John, that's why I'm forgetting everything. I hope I haven't been permanently damaged. All this time I thought I was doing the right thing by taking a sleeping pill rather than a pain pill so I could sleep. It's a miracle that we saw this program, and on the very night that I was telling you about my problems! I'll never take those pills again."

"It's strange," said John, "how you always seem to get a message when you have a problem."

"That's so true. I believe there's a spirit guide, an angel, or something watching over me. Let's hope they can heal my poor brain. I was about to forget my own name!"

After stopping the sleeping pills, I tested myself for days to see if I could concentrate or remember things. It wasn't long before I regained the abilities I had had before I started taking the pills. I thanked God for letting me know what was causing my problem and for restoring my mental functions.

The Car

57

The Car

In October 1989, six months after the rods had been removed, I decided I was ready to get a car that I could drive. My back pain was gone. I was thankful that I no longer had constant pain. I still had intermittent foot and leg pain, but I could tolerate that and seldom had to take pain pills. I felt that the pain would not be so severe that it would interfere with my driving. I was excited at the thought of driving again. I would finally be able to get away from the house on my own. I was anxious to pick out a car.

I needed a car that had enough space behind the driver's seat so that I could put my wheelchair there. Since the back door on four-door cars opened from the rear, I would have to choose a two-door car. I hoped to find one large enough that I could put the chair in, without having to take the wheels off. John and I had looked at many cars, but none had enough space behind the driver's seat to accommodate the wheelchair without taking the wheels off. I couldn't believe how difficult it was to get myself and the chair in a car.

I called Mobility Unlimited, a company that adjusts cars for disabled people, to see what they would recommend for me. They told me that there was no one car that was better than any other. Different people with different handicaps preferred different cars. I called several paraplegics that drive and found that their cars were different makes and sizes. One woman had a large old car with a single front seat. I didn't want an old car; I wanted one that would be dependable. Another drove a van. I didn't really want a van and I wouldn't have been able to get it down our driveway and into the garage. A son of two of our friends is in the car rental business and volunteered to find a car for me. After learning what I needed, Chuck checked with several car dealers. He called me to say that I might like an Oldsmobile Cutlass. They have a fairly large opening between the back of the driver's seat and the back of the door. My first thought was that I wasn't sure that I wanted an Oldsmobile. I had been riding in an Oldsmobile when I had had my accident. But I'm not superstitious. If that was the only car I could fit my chair in, then that's the car I would buy.

The next day my folks drove me to an Oldsmobile dealer. A salesman showed us the new 1989 Oldsmobile Cutlass. The car was beautiful, shiny and new. With the door open, I wheeled my chair next to the driver's seat and transferred onto the seat. It felt good to be behind the wheel of a car. It had been two and a half years since I had driven a car.

I thought, "With a car, I can be totally independent!"

Now that I was in the car, I had to get the chair in the back seat. I was afraid I might nick the car if I tried it, so I asked the salesman if he could put my chair in the back seat while I sat in the driver's seat. He put it in easily.

"Well," I thought, "if he can put it in easily, I'll be able to also. No problem."

When I got home, I called Chuck and told him the car was great. He said he would pick it up for me and have the hand control and a phone installed. When it was ready, he would deliver it to our home. I was so excited; I felt like a kid waiting for a new Christmas toy.

It took a week to have everything done. Chuck called to say that he would be driving the car to our home that day. After he arrived, he showed John and me how to use the hand control and the phone. He gave us manuals explaining how they worked. As soon as he left, I got into the driver's seat. The hand control stuck out horizontally, to the left of the wheel and below the turn signal. I practiced using it with the shift in neutral. It was simple enough. With my left hand I pressed down for acceleration and let up to slow down. By pushing the hand control forward, I could put on the brakes. Since I had to keep my left hand on the hand control, there was a steering knob on the wheel so I could turn the wheel with my right hand.

"Let's go for a drive," said John. "You can do it."

I slowly turned the key in the ignition and the motor started. Lights on the dash lit up. One said "Good afternoon." The clock showed me the day, date, and time. The temperature control had been set at 75 degrees. I thought, "This car is really fancy. It sure does a lot. I wonder if there's a button I can push so it will drive itself?"

I was as ready as I was going to be. I buckled up. I slowly pushed down on the hand control. I was nervous because I wasn't sure what would happen. The control was stiff, and when I finally pressed it down, the car jerked forward. I took my hand off the control thinking we would stop. The car kept rolling.

John yelled, "Push forward on the brake."

I finally braked to a stop. I took a deep breath and repeated to myself, "Down to go, forward to stop." With that in mind, I began again. It wasn't a smooth ride. I knew I was jerking John's head back and forth.

241

"John, I don't think I can do this."

"Yes, you can. It'll take some practice, but I know you can do it."

"Well, I hope I learn how before I kill us both. This seems harder than when I had to learn to shift."

I jolted and jerked my way down the street by the school. Since school was out and the parking lot was empty, John suggested that I practice in the parking lot. With some difficulty, I turned into the lot. In the lot and off the street, I felt more at ease. I didn't realize how difficult it would be to learn to accelerate and brake with my left hand while steering with my right. Every time I wanted to stop, I automatically tried to lift my right leg to push on the brake pedal. It was frustrating. I kept thinking, if I only had feeling in my feet so I could feel the pedals, I wouldn't need the hand control. I didn't always remember, down to go and forward to stop. When I wanted to turn, I would automatically put both hands on the wheel and try to put my foot on the brake pedal. When I took my hand off the control, the car kept moving.

"Push forward!" John would yell.

"Oh, John, this is terrible. I don't think I can drive this stupid car with just my hands. It's like rubbing my tummy and patting my head at the same time. I can't do that, either."

"Don't get discouraged. You'll do fine."

Poor John, even though his life was in danger, he had the patience of a saint. After a little more practice, I drove home. I was not happy with my first adventure in the car. It hadn't been what I had imagined it would be. I shouldn't have been surprised. Since my accident, I had frequently underestimated how difficult a task would be. Even the simplest thing takes lots of practice. Before the accident, I had taken so much for granted.

The next day, John encouraged me to drive the car to Foothills Tennis Club, about ten miles from our home. I was surprised that John was willing to go on another white knuckle ride. Although I was a little apprehensive, the trip to and from the club went smoothly. I was much encouraged.

One day I decided to practice getting the chair in and out of the car by myself. I was sure I could do it without too much trouble. John was always with me when I drove, and he would put the chair in the trunk before I drove and would take it out afterward. John would really be surprised when he came home and I could show him what I could do. I wheeled out to the garage, opened the car door, and transferred to the front seat of the car. Then I turned sideways and placed my feet firmly on the ground. To fold the chair I had to bend forward as far as I could. It wasn't easy, but I did it. The hard part was fitting the folded chair into the space behind the driver's seat. I got the small front wheels in, but I couldn't get the big back wheels in. I groaned and swore, but no matter how hard I struggled, it was simply impossible. I was frustrated and angry.

"All right," I said to myself. "Calm down and think this thing out." I decided I would have to take the wheels off the chair in order to get it in the back seat. I leaned over and removed each wheel, placing them one at a time on the back seat. Then I folded the frame of the chair. With much effort I was finally able to maneuver it into the space behind the driver's seat. It took much time, sweat, and tears. But I had done it. Now I had to get the chair frame out of the car and put the wheels on. I got the frame out and unfolded it without too much difficulty.

I had badly underestimated how difficult it would be to put the wheels on. Because the car had a broad "running board," I had to leave just a little of my fanny on the seat and lean way out to get my feet flat on the garage floor. I needed both hands to put the wheels on, and I couldn't keep my upper body steady without leaning on something. My frustration was increasing. I was in a very weak position. Bending forward and turning to the side was most uncomfortable. Trying to align the wheel pin with the hole hurt my arthritic fingers. After much fussing, swearing, and screaming, I was able to put one wheel on the chair. I couldn't move the chair into a position where I could get the second wheel on. I was determined to get that stupid wheel on even if it took all day. By this time I was so angry that I could hardly see through the tears. I thought that, if I could sit on the running board, I might be able to get the second wheel on. As I tried to lower myself, I slipped and fell onto the cement floor.

What a shock! I sat on the floor and looked upward.

"I hope you're enjoying yourself, Jesus. I can't understand why you're making my life so miserable!"

Sitting on the floor I found I could get the second wheel on the chair.

"I did it! As usual, it wasn't easy."

I turned over on my stomach, got up on my knees, and tried to pull myself up into the car. The garage floor was smooth cement, cold and slippery. Each time I tried to pull up, my legs and feet would slide out from under me. I kept trying with much irritation, swearing, yelling, and tears. I had multiple bruises. After about forty minutes had passed, with great determination, I finally was able to get into the front seat.

What a horrible experience! What a letdown! I had been so happy to get a new car and to drive it, imagining how much fun I would have and how independent I would be. Now I realized I couldn't get my stupid chair in and out of the car. I was crushed. I transferred into my chair and wheeled into the house. I called John at work. When I heard his voice, I fell apart. I sobbed, yelled, and rambled on. John couldn't understand me.

"Honey, what's wrong?" he asked.

"I FELL OUT OF THE DAMN CAR!" I yelled.

"How on earth did you do that?"

"IT WASN'T EASY."

"I don't understand. Maybe I should come home."

"What for? You can't do anything to help me," I cried.

"I'm sure you bruised yourself, and you may have other injuries. I'd better come home and check you out."

"Big deal, so what if I bruised myself. No sense you coming home just to look at my bruises. You can't fix them."

"Try to calm down, Babe. Tell me what you were doing in the car."

I started to cry. I explained that I wanted to surprise him by practicing putting my chair in the car by myself.

"I don't want you doing anything like that when I'm not home."

"How am I ever going to be independent if I always have to have someone around whenever I want to do something?"

"Babe, promise me you'll wait until I get home tonight and see if I can come up with some ideas."

"Okay," I grumbled. "I bet you won't be able to do it either."

"I'll see you in a little while. I love you, Babe. Be good till I get home!"

When John came home, he insisted on checking out my bruises. I had a fair number. John gave me a lecture about what was safe and what was unsafe behavior. He went out in the garage, sat in the driver's seat, and tried to get my chair in the back seat without taking the wheels off. He concluded it wasn't possible.

He wanted me to show him why I couldn't get the chair in and out with the wheels off. I didn't want to go out there again, but he persuaded me. When I sat in the front seat, he could see that the seat was too high and the car was too wide for me to safely take the wheels off or to put them on. I simply couldn't balance from that position. I had a car that wasn't right for me. I felt sorry for myself. Every time I thought about my fall, I became angry.

I kept thinking, "Everything I do is always so difficult. Screw the car. Who needs it? I'll stay home for the rest of my life." I was very emotional and dramatic.

The next morning, as I was lying in bed, Mom called.

"How are you feeling, Honey?" she asked.

"How do I feel? I'll tell you how I feel. I'm through with my therapy. I'm through with trying hard. I always try to have a good attitude, but what for? Nothing is easy any more. I can't even get in a stupid car. God is making my life miserable. He's probably up there laughing at me."

"Oh, honey, don't say that. God loves you."

"God doesn't love me. If He did, He would help me instead of making everything so hard."

"God does love you."

"Well, God can have my body if He wants it, and He can do whatever He wants with it. I'm not doing another thing.

246

I'm going to stay in bed for the rest of my life. I see no reason to get out of bed."

"Oh, Beverly, don't say things like that. There are a lot of reasons. I know you will get better. It just takes time."

"Mom, I've had it." I cried. "All my hard work, and for what? I don't feel like talking about it anymore. I'm going to go back to sleep."

"Daddy and I will stop by later on in the day and check on you. I love you. Bye."

I hung up the phone and grabbed my TV remote control. As long as I was going to spend the rest of my life in bed, I might as well watch the boob tube. It was a little after ten, and I knew "People Are Talking" was on. I turned on channel 5. I was amazed to hear what they were discussing. As guests, they had two paraplegics and a young man who was born without arms. One paraplegic told how he had climbed El Capitan in Yosemite. The other said that she had been a top ranked tennis player and a champion skier before her accident. Then they showed a video of her playing wheelchair tennis and skiing in a wheelchair.

"Everything I did before, I do now, only I do it in a different way," she said.

The young man with no arms happily played the guitar with his toes. He was fantastic. After he finished, people in the audience asked questions of the guests. One woman asked the young man if he missed not having arms.

His answer was, "Only when I want to hug someone."

My eyes filled with tears. I felt ashamed for feeling sorry for myself.

A question was directed to the young woman, "You seem so happy. Is there a special formula that you could share with us?"

"Actually, it's attitude. You can be unhappy and hide in bed for the rest of your life, or you can have a good attitude and enjoy life. It's really up to the individual."

I was totally embarrassed by how I had acted. Here are three handicapped people: one climbs a mountain, one owns her own business and plays tennis and skis, and the third is happy as can be doing everything with his feet and toes. Then there's me. I'm upset because I can't get my stupid chair in my car. How often I forget how lucky I am.

I sat up in bed, looked upward, and said, "Okay, I got the message. I know I shouldn't get so angry when things don't go right for me. I'll try not to complain anymore, but you have to remember, Jesus, I'm only human."

God works in strange ways. He always manages to get His message across. It was time for me to stop feeling sorry for myself. In five minutes I was dressed and out of bed.

"TODAY IS THE FIRST DAY OF THE REST OF MY LIFE," I thought.

From now on, things will be better.

10

The Driver
Who
Hit Us

58

The Driver Who Hit Us

After I came home from the hospital, many of my friends asked what had happened to the driver who hit us. I hadn't given him much thought and didn't know if he had gone to trial or not. I didn't know how to obtain any information.

After my accident, Stephanie had joined MADD and attended some of the meetings. She had been impressed by Jackie, the head of the San Jose chapter of MADD and suggested I call her.

I called Jackie to ask how I could get information about the man who had hit us. She suggested I call Charlene, the head of the Yucca Valley chapter of MADD.

Charlene was delightful and happy to help.

She found that the California Highway Patrol spokesman said the department initially recommended that the Riverside County district attorney's office file felony drunken driving and felony manslaughter charges against the driver.

Apparently, a blood sample for alcohol was not drawn from the driver until after he had been hospitalized and given medication and intravenous fluids. By that time, the blood alcohol was too low for him to be charged with drunk driving. He wasn't being charged with manslaughter either.

Charlene also told me that he had been repeatedly scheduled for court hearings, but for some reason, they had all been canceled. She said she would attend the next hearing in Palm Springs.

For nearly a year his hearings were repeatedly delayed. Charlene talked to the district attorney to find out what was happening. The D.A. said he would find out and call her.

The D.A. discovered that the judge who was hearing the case was a close friend of the driver's family. He asked for another judge to hear the case.

The driver of the truck did not own the truck. He was married, had no children, lived in an apartment, and had only a part-time job.

Charlene suggested that I write a letter to the new judge, telling him what my condition was and how it had affected me and my family. She also suggested that some of my friends write letters and tell of their feelings. Charlene wanted me to have all the letters mailed to her, so that she could personally deliver them to the judge. This had to be done before the next hearing, which was to be held in three days. A dozen letters from my friends and one from me were sent to Charlene by Federal Express.

The letter I sent:

Dear Ms. Messinese:

I can't understand why (the driver) has not been sentenced after all this time. The facts are clear and haven't changed. (He) was under the influence of alcohol and driving in a reckless manner, with no regard for the safety of others. He passed a car on the right and then drove over the centerstrip without braking, hitting our car head on. He killed two of my friends and badly injured another friend and me. The officers documented that he had been drinking and there were witnesses to the accident. How can he be sen-

tenced for anything less than manslaughter?

Does the judge understand the hell that (he) has put our four families through? Can he imagine what it's like to be hit head on, to be nearly cut in half by a seat belt, to have a friend vomit on you and die, or to be in such agonizing pain that you hoped you would die? Has the judge considered what it was like for me to go through two major abdominal surgeries, to have two long rods embedded in my back, to have a four inch bedsore which extends to the bone, to have urine come through a hole in my back, or to have a kidney removed?

Has he seen what it's like to have no bowel or bladder control? Does he know what it's like to have pain daily, which at times is so excruciating that it can't be controlled by narcotics and hypnosis? Can he imagine what effect my condition has on my parents, my husband, and my children?

(He) has not contacted any of our families to apologize or try to make amends for the tremendous damage that he has caused.

I have counseled my sons that it is wrong to take the law into one's own hands and that (he) is not worth going to prison for.

It seems obvious to me that (he) should spend as much time in prison as possible under the current laws of the state of California.

Sincerely,
Beverly Differding

After the hearing Charlene called to say that she had given the letters to the judge before the hearing. At the hearing the judge had been angry and had told the driver that he wished he could give him what he thought he deserved. The judge sentenced him to eight months in jail without parole, the maximum sentence under the law.

He loses eight months of freedom. Freedom for my two friends is gone forever, and I've lost the freedom to move as I did before.

Charlene told me that without the new judge and without the letters we had written, the case might have been dismissed.

It doesn't say much for our judicial system. A driver who had been drinking kills two people and seriously injures two, and we have to write letters so that his case isn't dismissed.

I hope eight months in jail gave him time to think about the pain he has caused to so many people. Hopefully, he will think twice before he drinks and drives.

The owner of the truck had $30,000 of insurance, which was split four ways, $7,500 for each victim and their families. John was contacted a month after the accident by Dee's lawyer, telling him about the insurance. John was under so much stress, he told him he didn't care about the money. But the lawyer suggested that John get his own lawyer so we would be able to get our share. John asked a tennis-playing friend of his to represent us. We discovered that our medical insurance company had a lien on any money that we collected from the party that was responsible for the accident. The medical insurance company received $5,000 and our attorney, $2,500.

Oh well, that's life!

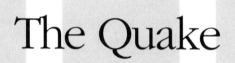

The Quake

59

The Quake

It was October 17, 1989 and a nice warm day. I had been working on maintaining a positive attitude, something that takes constant effort. For several weeks I had been trying to spend time writing on the computer. I had converted one bedroom into a combined library and computer room. The computer was on a table in front of the window, so that I could have a view while I thought about what I wanted to write. Against the wall behind me were three six-foot bookcases, and on my left was a five-foot high dresser. It was a comfortable room.

About six months ago, when John was filling the bookcases, I remember him saying, "I don't know if these bookcases are safe across from your computer. If we ever have an earthquake, and you're at the computer, get out of there. Those bookcases could injure you." I didn't give it much thought. I didn't often use the computer. We hadn't had an earthquake of any consequence since we had been in the house. I thought the odds must be a million to one that I would be there during a quake.

I sat down at the computer about four in the afternoon. John had called to tell me that he would be home about five. He usually calls to tell me when he is coming home, and he almost always is on time.

I was happy that I had about an hour to work on the computer. The sun was coming in the window. I was having a good day. Thoughts were flowing from my mind easily and I was writing them all down.

A little after five the phone rang. Shortly after I said hello, I heard a loud noise like a huge truck. It quickly got louder, and then the whole room began to shake.

I yelled into the phone, "It's an earthquake! My God, it's an earthquake!"

As the room shook, I dropped the phone. I remembered that John had said to get out of the room. I quickly wheeled back from the table so I could turn toward the door. The roar was frightening. The room was moving so much that my chair hit the dresser. I couldn't back away from it. The dresser was wobbling, and I put my hands up to keep it from falling on me. The noise was so loud that I couldn't hear myself screaming. I was petrified. A wooden duck and other things on top of the dresser fell down around me. I heard books hit the floor. Out of the corner of my eye, I saw the bookcases falling. I couldn't get out of the way, and I knew I was going to get hit.

Then I felt as if someone had pushed my shoulders forward. I was leaning over the front of my chair as far as the dresser would allow, when the bookcase hit the back of my chair and grazed my upper back. One of the handholders on the chair knocked out the back of the bookcase. The rest of the bookcase was lying on the chair so I couldn't move the chair at all. The floor was violently shaking, and I thought the house would come down. I kept screaming. I tried to keep from falling by pushing against the dresser.

Suddenly, I was thrown off the left side of the chair onto the floor. The chair was wedged between the bookcase and the table, and my right foot was caught between the dresser and the chair. I couldn't get my foot free. Finally, the house stopped shaking. I kept twisting my foot with both hands and, after some pushing and pulling, was finally able to get it free. I couldn't move my chair. I saw that one of the bookcases had come down so fast that all of the books were still in it. The room was a mess. I felt another tremor. As fast as I could, I crawled out of the room and down the hall. The living room was covered with broken glass and china that had fallen out of the cabinet. I reached the front door, unlocked it, opened it, and crawled outside onto the ramp.

I yelled, "Help!" over and over. A neighbor heard me and rushed to my rescue. I asked her to see if she could get my chair. It took her a few minutes to get it free and bring it outside. She helped me into it. She brought me my portable phone. Then she had to leave to check on her children.

I waited on the ramp for John to come. He was late, and I was concerned. As I sat there, I could feel aftershocks. I hung onto my chair for fear I would be thrown off again.

I called my folks in San Jose. They were all right and said they would come over right away. I phoned my daughter-in-law, Stephanie, in Davis. She, my son Gary, and their daughter were all right. The quake hadn't done any damage there. While I was on the phone, my stepdaughter, Amy, called to be sure I was all right. Then Stephanie kept me on the phone until John got home.

It wasn't till six o'clock that John arrived. He had been in the basement of his medical clinic when the quake hit. He had tried to call me right away, but the phone lines were dead. He left immediately, but found slow traffic everywhere. Traffic lights were out, there were some traffic accidents, some telephone and power wires were down, and one street was flooded by a broken water main. He had been fortunate to get home in an hour, a trip that usually takes twenty minutes. Soon my folks arrived. The house was in a terrible state. Six of the seven bookcases had fallen. One had broken a leg on the computer table. Fortunately, the computer and printer had been shoved against the window sill and had not fallen off the table. One of the bookcases had broken the back of the chair at John's desk. Surprisingly, the only bookcase with glass windows had not fallen.

All of the china and crystal had fallen out of the cabinet and were shattered on the living room floor. There were cracks running from two doorways to the ceiling and a crack had opened on the ceiling over the hallway. Cracks extended down from the corners of the frames of three of the windows.

In the kitchen many of the dishes and glasses had fallen out of the cupboards. On the floor was a combination of **glass, Ragu sauce, flour, and sugar. In the garage the ladder** and a piece of plywood had fallen against the new car and shattered the back window. Many things had fallen off the shelves. Fortunately, Mandy had been in the backyard and hadn't been injured. If she had been with me, she would probably have been injured by one of the bookcases. If she had been in the kitchen she might have been cut by the glass. She was afraid to come into the house.

I had bruises on my left side and a large one on my right foot. I had taken some skin off my right ankle when I had pulled it out from under the chair, but nothing that wouldn't heal. My stepdaughter, Joan, called to be sure we were all right. It was difficult trying to clean up with only candles and flashlights, but we had most of it cleaned up that evening. Occasional aftershocks were not reassuring. I sometimes thought I felt tremors, even when the light fixtures weren't swaying. After my folks had helped as much as they could, they went home.

We weren't upset with all the damage. We were happy that all of our family was safe, and that it hadn't been worse. I had survived again.

The Move

12

60

The Move

After the quake I was bothered by the thought that I couldn't wheel up our steep driveway to the street. I felt trapped in our house. John and I decided we should move.

I called my friend Lynn, who works for a realty company, and three days later I met with Lynn and her employer, Lois. I liked Lois. I told her what we could afford and the kind of home I thought I would need.

Several days later Lynn called. She asked if she and Lois could pick me up and show me some homes they thought I would like. I was excited and thought house hunting would be fun.

The first day wasn't. I was unable to get my wheelchair into any of the homes. I had to be wheeled around the outside and look through the windows. I was discouraged. I wouldn't buy a house without looking at it from the inside.

Lynn offered to buy a portable ramp for me, and I agreed. That evening she brought me the ramp, which looked like two collapsible lightweight metal skis that could be extended to a length of six feet. I was anxious to try them.

The next day Lois and Lynn were able to wheel me up the ramp into a house that we had previously visited. As we went through each room, they told me what I could do to decorate it to my liking.

"You could hang something here." "You could place

plants on this shelf." "You could go to this special little shop and pick up some great looking baskets."

As they talked, I realized I couldn't stand up to hang pictures or put plants on shelves. It wouldn't be easy for me to shop for baskets. I was depressed. Moving seemed impossible.

That evening I told John what had happened and started to cry. I felt frustrated and useless.

Remodeling and redecorating our old home seemed far easier than moving. I would have to live with my steep driveway and little view of the street above. I called Lois to thank her for her time. I explained my frustration. She understood.

I decided to replace my front door and several sliding closet doors. I made arrangements for someone to come to the house and give me an estimate. The man told me the work would start in two weeks.

Several weeks later, when no one had come, I called the company and left a message on their recorder. Days passed without a return call. The fourth time I called the company, I told them to forget it, I would have someone else do the work.

I called another company. Again I was told that the work would be done in two weeks, and again I never heard from them. I couldn't believe how inconsiderate these people were. After two months, nothing had been done. I dropped that project.

I decided to buy a few new pieces of furniture and reupholster my dining room chairs.

When Lynn came by, I told her about trying to replace my doors. I joked that, "Maybe somebody's trying to tell me something."

"They're probably telling you to move out of this house.

It bothers me to see you in this house with no way to get to the street. I wish you'd think about moving."

"I don't know, Lynn. All the effort of looking at homes and all the trouble of moving seems so difficult. Nothing is easy for me."

"How about listing those things that you would like in a house? Lois and I will only call you when we find something that fits your needs."

"I'm still not sure I want to move."

"Promise you'll make out a list for me," smiled Lynn.

"Okay," I promised.

That evening I listed what I wanted:

> *(1) Flat ground from the house to the street.*
> *(2) A six foot fence in the backyard for our dog.*
> *(3) Hardwood floors so it would be easier on my hands to wheel through the house.*
> *(4) Wide doorways that I could get my chair through easily.*
> *(5) A newer home requiring less repair work.*
> *(6) A modern kitchen.*
> *(7) A bathroom wide enough that I could turn my chair and face the sink.*
> *(8) Rooms brightened by daylight and sunshine.*
> *(9) A jacuzzi.*

I drew a happy face and chuckled to myself. I doubted there was a house with all these ingredients. I showed John my list.

"You don't want much," he said with a smile.

"I can dream can't I? Why wish for a slice of bread when you can wish for the whole loaf?"

The next morning Lois called to say she had the perfect house for me.

"But you haven't even seen my list yet," I said.

"I'll pick you up in fifteen minutes."

I wasn't prepared to look at a house. I hurried to get ready. Lynn and Lois arrived and drove me to my "perfect house." They set up the ramp and wheeled me inside. As I entered, I knew this was going to be my new home. I didn't need to see the rest of the house to know. It was going to be mine.

As I wheeled in and out of each room, I became more excited.

"I've got to call John and have him stop by on his way home from work. Would that be possible?" I asked.

"You bet. We can meet him here about five o'clock."

I was so happy. When I returned home, I called John to tell him about the wonderful house. He sounded skeptical, but agreed to stop at the house on his way home.

I met him there. Once inside he was impressed.

"What do you think, Hon?" I asked.

"I can't believe it, Babe. It has all the things on your list, including a jacuzzi in the bathroom!"

Until John mentioned it, I had forgotten about the list. We looked at each other in amazement. The house had everything I wanted, and John liked it too.

We asked Lois if we could make an offer on the house that day. She suggested we return to our home and draw up the papers. She would call the owners later that evening. The process didn't take long. We signed the papers and Lois made arrangements to meet with the owners. She returned with good and bad news. They had accepted our offer, but we had to have the cash in two weeks.

"My word, Lois, how can we come up with that amount of cash in so short a time? We have to sell our home first."

"Don't worry, Bev," said Lois. "We'll put your house up for sale on Monday. This is only Friday, so you'll have Saturday and Sunday to get it ready to show."

She showed us listings of the homes in our area and pointed out that most of them were taking months to sell. She suggested that our asking price be lower than that of comparable homes in our area so that we had a better chance of selling it quickly. We agreed.

By Monday morning I was ready. At nine o'clock Lois came with a FOR SALE sign. Lynn brought beautiful potted flowers to place in the front of the house and in the entrance way. By ten o'clock many realtors from different companies were touring the house and seemed pleased. Some told me they thought it would sell soon. Others asked if they could bring their clients by that afternoon. I called John to tell him of the positive response we received.

"I think we should have asked for more," said John.

"Oh, John, don't be greedy."

"You don't understand," he said. "You can always come down on your price, but once the price is listed, you can't go up."

"Don't worry, hon, if God wants us to have more money we'll get more."

By late Tuesday afternoon four couples were interested in buying our home. We met with each couple at Lois' office.

The first three couples offered to pay what we asked. To get the house, the last couple offered us more than the asking price.

John looked at me, shook his head, and said, "I can't believe you. Somebody up there is watching out for you."

"No, John, they're watching out for both of us."

"No way, I'm just a spectator."

We sold and bought a house within five days. It was meant to be.

Before we moved in, I measured all the rooms and drew a floor plan. I measured the furniture and knew where each piece would fit. I could tell the movers where to place each piece of furniture.

March 29th we moved into our new home, just six weeks after we made our offer. Packing, moving, and settling in the new home went smoothly.

I was amazed how much I could do on my own. I even hung some of my pictures. It only took us a few days to unpack all the boxes.

Each day I can sit in my kitchen and look out the window at the flowers, the birds in the fruit trees, and watch people and animals pass by. I wait for the mailtruck so I can wheel outside, past the flowers, to the mail box and bring in the mail, something I couldn't do at the old house.

The house is perfect for me.

Epilogue

Epilogue

I've learned some important lessons.

As I look back on my Egypt, Palm Springs, and earthquake misadventures, I realize how accurate my intuition was. I don't need a psychic to tell me what I should or shouldn't do. I need only listen to my inner self. It's surprising how many of us seek answers from friends and strangers rather than looking inside ourselves.

Life was easy before my accident. Since the accident I've often been in excruciating pain. Recovery has been slow, frustrating, and discouraging. But I have survived and at times flourished. This time has not been wasted. I have painted, had art showings, written this book, spoken to the Rotary Club, been interviewed on cable TV, and found a new home.

Although the accident has taken away some physical mobility, it has given me a richer life. I no longer concern myself with the past or worry about the future. I live in the now. I have learned to appreciate life and all its beauty.

I have learned how to use self-hypnosis to cope with severe pain. Using visualization I realized what control the mind has over healing. The courage I needed to get through this difficult time came from within me.

I believe the mind is so powerful that, if you use it to its fullest, you can do almost anything. Not just thinking it or saying it, but wanting it, picturing it, and believing, without doubt, that it will happen. You must live your life preparing for it to happen.

Since I left the hospital, my physical progress has been amazing. Initially, I had almost no feeling from the waist down. About 80% of the feeling has returned, and I am still improving. I can move my legs enough to walk with a walker. Compared to my physician's predictions, my improvement has been miraculous. My goal is to strengthen the muscles I have, so I can walk further and possibly, someday, walk without a walker.

I believe we are put on earth to enhance our spiritual growth. The difficulties we encounter are part of our learning. How we handle them enables us to grow. We must listen to our bodies and be in tune with our inner self. My visions, out-of-body experiences, healings, and meaningful dreams all come from a higher consciousness, and whether we call them psychic or spiritual, it's all the same. Something more powerful, more knowing, and more loving is there for those who will take the time to listen and allow themselves to believe. We must strive for unconditional love, for, with love, one can perform miracles.

I thank God for surrounding me with love, for giving me the strength to continue, and for letting me know that I will walk again.

I continue to improve. I must be patient. With time, I will be healed.

ORDER FORM

Please send____ copy(s) of With Love, Bev
1 Book @ $14.95 ea.
Shipping $_____ (Add $3.10 per book)
Subtotal $_____
Tax $_____ (CA residents only add 8.25 %)
Total $_____

Name_____
Address_____
City_____
State_____ Zip_____

Make check or money order payable to and mail to:
Gander Publishing
553 Thain Way
Palo Alto, CA. 94306